Management Extra

MAKING SENSE
OF DATA AND
INFORMATION

Management Extra

MAKING SENSE OF DATA AND INFORMATION

ELSEVIER

eLEARN

Pergamon
Flexible
Learning

AMSTERDAM • BOSTON • HEIDELBERG • LONDON • NEW YORK • OXFORD • PARIS •
SAN DIEGO • SAN FRANCISCO • SINGAPORE • SYDNEY • TOKYO

Pergamon Flexible Learning is an imprint of Elsevier
Linacre House, Jordan Hill, Oxford OX2 8DP, UK
30 Corporate Drive, Suite 400, Burlington, MA 01803, USA

First edition 2007

British Library Cataloguing in Publication Data
A catalogue record for this book is available from the British Library

Library of Congress Cataloging-in-Publication Data
A catalog record for this book is available from the Library of Congress

ISBN: 978-0-08-046521-0

For information on all Pergamon Flexible Learning publications visit
our web site at books.elsevier.com

Printed and bound in Italy

07 08 09 10 11 10 9 8 7 6 5 4 3 2 1

Contents

Activities

Figures

Tables

Series preface

Whether you are a tutor/trainer or studying management development to further your career, Management Extra provides an exciting and flexible resource helping you to achieve your goals. The series is completely new and up-to-date, and has been written to harmonise with the 2004 national occupational standards in management and leadership. It has also been mapped to management qualifications, including the Institute of Leadership & Management's middle and senior management qualifications at Levels 5 and 7 respectively on the revised national framework.

For learners, coping with all the pressures of today's world, Management Extra offers you the flexibility to study at your own pace to fit around your professional and other commitments. Suddenly, you don't need a PC or to attend classes at a specific time – choose when and where to study to suit yourself! And, you will always have the complete workbook as a quick reference just when you need it.

For tutors/trainers, Management Extra provides an invaluable guide to what needs to be covered, and in what depth. It also allows learners who miss occasional sessions to 'catch up' by dipping into the series.

This series provides unrivalled support for all those involved in management development at middle and senior levels.

Reviews of Management Extra

I have utilised the Management Extra series for a number of Institute of Leadership and Management (ILM) Diploma in Management programmes. The series provides course tutors with the flexibility to run programmes in a variety of formats, from fully facilitated, using a choice of the titles as supporting information, to a tutorial based programme, where the complete series is provided for home study. These options also give course participants the flexibility to study in a manner which suits their personal circumstances. The content is interesting, thought provoking and up-to-date, and, as such, I would highly recommend the use of this series to suit a variety of individual and business needs.

Martin Davies BSc(Hons) MEd CEngMIMechE MCIPD FITOL FInstLM
Senior Lecturer, University of Wolverhampton Business School

At last, the complete set of books that make it all so clear and easy to follow for tutor and student. A must for all those taking middle/senior management training seriously.

Michael Crothers, ILM National Manager

Making sense of data and information

How can you turn data into meaningful information and actionable knowledge? This is a question that challenges many managers. We work in a society where we are exposed to quite staggering volumes of data, some of it conflicting and not all of it true.

As a manager you need to be able to make sense of the data and to use it selectively to answer key questions: Why has quality fallen in the last week? Should we subcontract or employ more people? What will consumer demand be in the future? You need to be able to assess the value of data and to detect what is and what isn't spin.

This book explores how you can use data to help you make timely, accurate and smarter business decisions.

The focus is on analysing numbers. On their own, figures tell you very little. To become meaningful they need to be processed and analysed and it is the patterns that emerge from this that provide the information you need for decision-making.

The book is arranged in four themes. You start by considering the value of information in organisations and by assessing how effectively you use information in your management role.

You then go on to look at different options for presenting figures so that trends become clearer and patterns simpler to spot. As well as making data easier to interpret, the techniques you explore are valuable communication tools that will help you use information more effectively with others.

The last two themes then provide a toolkit of techniques that you can use to investigate situations and help solve problems. These include statistical and operational techniques as well as computer tools. Like any toolkit, the key to using it properly lies in knowing not only what each tool does but when to use it. This book will help you to develop this ability by applying the methods that are described within a business context.

Your objectives are to:

- **appraise how effectively you use information to inform decision making and improvement**
- **explore how you can use graphical techniques and other visual tools to make data more accessible and easier to analyse**
- **enhance your ability to use data to construct and present a persuasive argument**

- assess the uses, benefits and limitations of spreadsheets in analysing and presenting data

- identify how analytical statistics and operational research techniques can be applied to solve business problems.

Becoming a critical thinker

Why are some people better than others at problem solving and decision making? One important characteristic that differentiates effective decision makers is their ability to think critically. Managers who are critical thinkers use information , both qualitative and quantitative, to help arrive at and to present the most reasonable and justifiable position that is possible.

To many of us the numbers can be a turn off. We can deal with headlines like a 70% increase, but after that our interest begins to wane. The danger is that we accept things at face value rather than try to untangle the numbers to gain a truer picture. Consider the following:

Sleight of statistic

Headline: 5,000 extra police pledged
In actual fact: This will replace those leaving the force

Headline: £50m promised to fight heart disease
In actual fact: This was part of the £21bn already pledged to the Health Service

Headline: £21bn for the Health Service
In actual fact: Spread over 3 years

Source: www.bbc.co.uk

Critical thinking involves acquiring information and evaluating it to reach a well justified conclusion. This doesn't mean collecting information exhaustively. Collecting information can be costly and time-consuming. Some information may not be available, because of Data Protection for example, or because it is held by a competitor. We need the skills to decide when we have sufficient information, and when obtaining further information is impracticable or unnecessary.

This first theme begins by looking at the role information plays in effective management and at the sources of data you use. It ends by exploring the concept of critical thinking in more detail. Rather than trusting that things will turn out right, we'll explain the benefits of carefully following a logical process and critically checking your thoughts, actions and decisions at every stage.

In this theme you will:

◆ **identify the information needs of your team and assess how effectively these are being met**

◆ **critically consider the factors that affect the quality and use of data and information**

♦ gather and record information relevant to your own area of responsibility, complying with any constraints on the collection of, and access to, data

♦ explore the characteristics of critical thinking and assess your own critical thinking skills.

Why we need information

> **"Errors using inadequate data are much less than those using no data at all."**
> **Charles Babbage**

At the heart of any management system you need good decisions and good information. In his book on Leadership, Rudy Guiliani, ex-mayor of New York tells how timely access to accurate information helped improve decision making in New York City's fight against crime.

Back in the early nineties, the scale of crime in New York was immense. "We were looking at 9000-10000 felonies a week and anywhere from 1800-2000 murders per year. Evaluating the data annually or even quarterly wasn't telling us anything. By the time a pattern was noticed, it would have changed. It was anyone's guess whether say a pattern of three AM gas robbers was emerging."

Compstat (an abbreviation of "computer comparison statistics") was an innovation of the New York City Police Department designed to make information available instantly. As each report was logged by a Police Officer it was plotted onto a computer-generated citywide map showing where and when crime was occurring. With 'real time' access to information on the victim, time of occurrence, and other crime-specific details police were able to identify trouble spots and target the appropriate resources to fight crime strategically. The impact was immediate and revolutionary. Major felonies fell 12.3% in the year following its introduction and soon lay below that in other American cities.

Source: Adapted from Guiliani (2003)

Information for decision making

Whether in their immediate impact or their long term significance, some decisions are undoubtedly more important than others and require more time and more resource. One way to think about decisions is to look at them at three levels:

◆ **Operational decisions** are the day-to-day decisions affecting the running of the organisation. The decisions tend to be short term (days or weeks), routine and need to be made quite frequently. For example, a supermarket deciding on whether it needs to order more strawberries to cope with current demand. The consequences of a bad operational decision will be minimal, although a *series* of bad or sloppy operational decisions can cause harm.

◆ **Tactical decisions** have a longer time frame (months or years) and tend to have moderate consequences. For example, a toy shop timing the start of its Christmas promotion.

◆ **Strategic decisions** affect the organisational plans of the whole business, possibly for a number of years, and so are made less frequently. For example, whether to sell off a subsidiary company in response to falling profits. These decisions are the most risky, partly because they reach so far into the future and partly because they are of such importance.

All these decisions will require information, but the type and volume of information that is needed will be different for each level of decision making. See Figure 1.1.

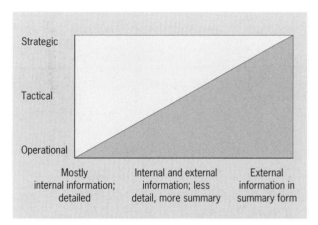

Figure 1.1 *Characteristics of information for management decisions*

Source: Nickerson (2001)

Operational decisions rely mostly on detailed data that is generated internally; how many strawberries did we sell yesterday, or last weekend? Operational decisions are often proceduralised by setting up information systems to capture performance data e.g. a stock control system. Decisions are usually low-cost because they can be made quickly with the minimum of effort.

Tactical decisions involve collating a wider spread of information that is relevant to the problem: for the past two years, what were the sales figures for the month prior to the Christmas promotion and during the promotion? When are other stores starting their promotion?

Strategic decisions are the most uncertain and high cost to make. Because of their impact they usually demand information from a number of sources. These will include performance figures from inside the organisation, but also far more external information in the form of financial forecasts and analyses from the wider marketplace, its own shareholders' views, and so on.

Do notice, however, that all of these decisions will inevitably be linked. For example, if a supermarket has made a strategic decision to maximise its payments to shareholders, it may make a linked tactical decision to delay the introduction of a new products delivery system, and this may itself make it difficult for local managers to make operational decisions to change stock levels when there is a change in the weather.

How good are management decisions?

Informix, a software development company, carried out a survey in 1999 to examine how decisions are made in different organisations around the world, and to find out how well the available information, in all its forms, supported the decision-making process.

A general finding was that managers, even when they are supported by a multitude of different information sources, find decision making extremely stressful. Most of these managers quoted examples of major decisions that were made incorrectly in the previous six months, and the larger the organisation, the more likely it was to have had a problem.

Among the most important negative effects on decision making was using limited, incorrect or misinterpreted data.

Some key findings of the survey:

◆ 32 per cent of the sample had made an important business decision in the past six months based on hope or luck.

◆ 33 per cent of managers ignore relevant data either when making a decision in the first place or when it becomes apparent that a decision has been incorrect.

◆ the single biggest cause of stress in decision making is a lack of information.

Source: *Informix* (1999)

What information do you need?

Without a good flow of information, most organisations would not find it possible to function, and all organisations will have information systems of some kind even if they are relatively informal. Information systems have evolved radically in recent years to mirror changes in organisations and the business context and to take advantage of advancing technologies. This has had an impact on how people use information.

◆ Organisations have become flatter and moved towards fluid, team based structures and project environments. These operate with reporting structures and information systems that look more like a net than a tree. Information systems are focused on getting information to the people who need it rather than passing information up and down the line of management command.

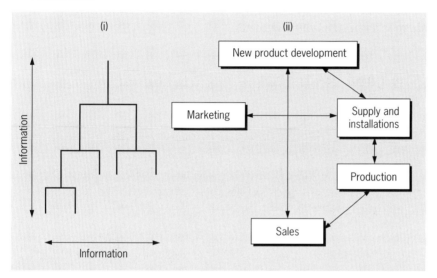

Figure 1.2 *Information flow in i) a hierarchy and ii) a project based organisation*

◆ New media (particularly electronic media) have made it possible to communicate information faster and more directly and through many more channels. From e-mail to pagers and mobile phones, PDA's, wikis and Intranets, the options to present information through different channels and formats is now immense.

◆ With the explosion of electronic information, information has become more readily available and far exceeds that which most organisations or its people can handle. Instead of information being pushed to the users, the new rule is to expect the users to pull information from the system when they need it.

The impact, as a manager, is that you need to manage information flows proactively, rather than rely on the systems. You need to know what information you and your team need and how to get it, and you need to know what information other people need from you and be able to provide it. This means regularly assessing information flows into and out of your team.

Activity 1
Your contribution to the information flow in your organisation

Objective

To analyse the way in which information flows in and out of your team.

Task

Mapping the information flows into and out of your team is one way to think about how effectively you manage information. To do this you need to identify the people who supply you and your team with information, and the people who require information from you.

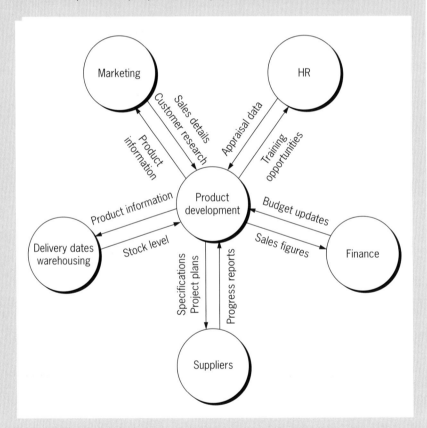

Figure 1.3 *Information map*

1. Draw a similar map to show how information flows to and from you and your team. Highlight on your map the key information that is important to you achieving your objectives.

2. Now think about how effectively this information meets your decision making needs. And conversely, how well you are meeting the information needs of others within and outside your organisation. Summarise any barriers you have identified below and identify what you might do to remove them.

Barriers	Possible actions for improvement
Information that my team receives	

Information that my team provides

Feedback

You probably found that some of the information that you use and/or provide passes through formal systems and some through informal channels. On the map you might like to highlight which channels are formal and which are informal.

Formal systems tend to be structured systems that have a fixed purpose. Examples might include a stock control system. Formal systems tend to be managed by a strict set of rules and to require specific inputs (e.g. barcode scans) to create pre-defined outputs (e.g. stock control reports). One of the most common barriers in a formal system is whether the output is in a format that is useful to you. This can be difficult and expensive to change and despite enormous investments in systems design, the rapidly changing business environment means that it is often difficult for formal information systems to mirror business practice.

Far more information passes informally. This includes information that passes by email, voicemail, computer conferencing, searching in databases, surveys, internet searches and the list could go on. People sometimes prefer informal systems because the response is instant and the information can be tailored to meet your specific needs. The process is quicker and so it may feel more efficient than a formal system, but as a user you need to keep in mind that informal communication systems are far more susceptible to human fallibility. The information may be incomplete, inaccurate or arrive too late for you to make a decision at all. Poor information leads to poor decisions, potentially worse than those made with no information at all. The ability to judge the credibility of information is central to your effectiveness as a critical thinker and decision maker. We look more at this later in this theme.

We noted earlier that rather than push information around, there is a move to make individuals responsible for 'pulling' information from systems when they need it. The most obvious example is the Intranet but you might have identified other examples in your own map. It's blindingly obvious but unless you know how to find and access the information that you need, it may as well not exist. To hone your decision making skills you need to be able to navigate your organisation's information systems – both formal and informal.

Using data, information and knowledge

Information systems might differ wildly in form and application but essentially they serve a common purpose which is to convert data into meaningful information which in turn enables the organisation to build knowledge:

◆ **Data** is unprocessed facts and figures without any added interpretation or analysis. "The price of crude oil is $80 per barrel."

◆ **Information** is data that has been interpreted so that it has meaning for the user. "The price of crude oil has risen from $70 to $80 per barrel" gives meaning to the data and so is said to be information to someone who tracks oil prices.

◆ **Knowledge** is a combination of information, experience and insight that may benefit the individual or the organisation. "When crude oil prices go up by $10 per barrel, it's likely that petrol prices will rise by 2p per litre" is knowledge.

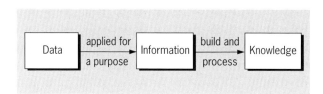

Figure 1.4 *From data to information to knowledge*

The boundaries between the three terms are not always clear. What is data to one person is information to someone else. To a commodities trader for example, slight changes in the sea of numbers on a computer screen convey messages which act as information that enables a trader to take action. To almost anyone else they would look like raw data. What matters are the concepts and your ability to use data to build meaningful information and knowledge.

Converting data into information

Data becomes information when it is applied to some purpose and adds value for the recipient. For example a set of raw sales figures is data. For the Sales Manager tasked with solving a problem of poor sales in one region, or deciding the future focus of a sales drive, the raw data needs to be processed into a sales report. It is the sales report that provides information.

In the first column below you'll see some examples of the huge amount of data that managers may receive. The second column then shows how the various types of data could be processed to create useful information.

Data	Possible methods of converting data into information
Sales figures	Plot charts and identify trends
Market and competition data	Find average or typical values
Financial performance	Present complex data as a chart or graph
Production output	Monitor changes over time and forecast future values
Costs of resources or other inputs	Compare figures and identify similarities or differences
Staff absences, holidays or sick leave	Assess whether a result is significant or occurred by chance
Accident records	Assess whether one thing is related to another.

Table 1.1 *Converting data to information*

Collecting data is expensive and to merit the effort, you need to be very clear about why you need it and how you plan to use it. One of the main reasons that organisations collect data is to monitor and improve performance. Measure what matters might be a bit of a cliché but if you are to have the information you need for control and performance improvement, you need to:

◆ collect data on the indicators that really do affect performance

◆ collect data reliably and regularly

◆ be able to convert data into the information you need.

Here are some perspectives from CEOs on the indicators that they track. Read their comments and then decide for yourself. What are the measurements that matter to you?

> There are few metrics to which I pay closer attention than "system uptime" -- how often Sun systems are up and running at customer sites. The most important commitment that we can make as a company is to share our customers' risk. Most of our customers face the same risk: computer systems that go down when people need them.

Scott McNealy, President and CEO of Sun MicroSystems

> I monitor costs because being low-cost is the core of our business strategy. The rationale behind an airline like Go is that keeping costs low lets us offer customers a cheaper way to fly -- and, as a result, more people will want to travel.

Barbara Cassani, ex CEO of Go Fly (now part of EasyJet)

We are a service organization. Our customers are the citizens of Charleston. In my 17 years as head of this organization, the question that I've always asked myself is, "are citizens happy with the job that we're doing?" One metric I use to answer that question is the number of complaints that we receive. Complaints provide a window into your overall performance. When one citizen makes a complaint, four or five others probably feel the same way but either don't take the time to complain or don't think that it would do any good.

Reuben Greenberg, Chief of police,
Charleson Police Department, South Carolina.

The difference between a great technology company and an average technology company is how much intellectual property a company creates. I keep a close eye on two measurements. One is our rate of innovation in existing products. I want to know how many customer-requested features are making it into the next release. The other measurement that I track is patent flow.

Edward Iacobucci, Founder, chairman, and CTO, Citrix Systems Inc.

Source: www.fastcompany.com

To be useful, data must also satisfy a number of conditions. It must be:

♦ **relevant** to the specific purpose

♦ **complete**

♦ **accurate**

♦ **timely**; data that arrives after you have made your decision is of no value

♦ **in the right format**; information can only be analysed using a spreadsheet if all the data can be entered into the computer system

♦ **available at a suitable price**; the benefits of the data must merit the cost of collecting or buying it.

The same criteria apply to information. Throughout this book you will repeatedly see the importance of:

♦ getting the right information

and

♦ getting the information right.

A manager investigating poor punctuality of trains on a particular line needs information showing all the arrival data on that line. Data on other lines is irrelevant, unless late connections elsewhere are causing the problem. Just as important, the manager must use the data correctly. One day of engineering works will have a major impact on a week's results. Wrongly interpreting the results could identify a problem where no problem actually exists.

Converting information to knowledge

Ultimately the tremendous amount of information that is generated is only useful if it can be applied to create knowledge within the organisation. Building and managing knowledge is one of the greatest challenges that faces organisations in the twenty first century. We hear a lot about the knowledge economy and for many organisations it is their knowledge or 'know how' that defines their competitive advantage.

There is considerable blurring and confusion between the terms 'information' and 'knowledge'. It is helpful to think of knowledge as being of two types:

♦ **Formal, explicit or generally available knowledge**. This is knowledge that has been captured and used to develop policies and operating procedures for example.

♦ **Instinctive, subconscious, tacit or hidden knowledge**. Within the organisation there are certain people who hold specific knowledge or have the 'know how' – "I did something very similar to that last year and this happened….."

Clearly, both types of knowledge are essential for the organisation.

A systematic approach to information management

When you want a sandwich for lunch, do you buy the one wrapped roughly in cling film or the one that is carefully packaged, looks more appetising but costs more? Quality, design and branding are important factors in determining price. It is true for trivial purchases but also for major ones such as cars. Consider the following saloons, the Kia Magentis costs £14495 and the Audi A4 25% more at £19875. On the face of it these two cars are very similar:

Model	Length	Width	Top speed	0-60mph	Mpg	Co2/tax %
Kia Magentis 2.0 4 door	474	181	129	10.2	36.7	192/26%
Audi A4 2.0 4 door	445	177	131	9.9	34.9	185/24%

Source: Top Gear

From the customer point of view the price suggests that the Audi represents a far more attractive combination of raw materials than the Kia. Starting with the same kinds of inputs (and similar amounts of labour and materials), Audi add more value or build in more 'know how' than Kia. Know-how of course includes different types of information, for instance design information, production information as well as the tacit knowledge of Audi's staff. Presumably the manufacturers at Kia would like to know how to produce a car that they can charge more for and so it's reasonable to assume that they face an important challenge on how to manage their information and use it more effectively to build knowledge and capability in their organisation.

Source: Adapted from Wilson (2002)

Information on its own will not create a knowledge-based organisation but it is a key building block. The right information fuels the development of intellectual capital which in turns drives innovation and performance improvement.

Activity 2
Using data and information to make a difference

Objective

This activity will help you to consider how effectively you use data and information to measure performance in your business area.

Task

Earlier you looked at how a number of CEO's use indicators to track performance in their organisation. e.g. costs in a low cost airline. Simple measures have an important influence on behaviour – what gets measured gets done. They also indicate issues for you to explore further e.g. Why did sales figures surge (or conversely, plummet) last month?

Think about your team or business area. Identify the key processes that you carry out. Focus on the one or two processes that are really important to the achievement of your objectives. Now think about how you measure how well these processes are working. What data do you capture and how do you translate that into information that you can share with your team?

Make some notes in the table below:

Process	What are the key indicators of performance?	What data do you capture ?	How is this translated into information to share with your team ?	How effective is the information? What improvements would you suggest?
A consultancy team delivers training design services to corporate clients.	Client satisfaction is a key measure of performance as are the number of fee-earning days completed per month to ensure that the team meets its financial targets.	Data is captured through client feedback sessions and from the completed time sheets of consultants.	Data is summarised into reports that are shared with the consultants at team meetings.	The information is timely and accurate. Customer feedback shows whether the customer was happy with the service but not whether they went onto purchase further business. Need to incorporate repeat business into the report.

Feedback

Completing this activity emphasises that both you and your team members need data and information to operate and measure how effectively you are operating. In relation to the performance data that you collect, you'll also need to consider whether you are measuring what matters. You can do this by identifying the information you need in order to achieve your objectives. Collecting too much information might be expensive and render you liable to information overload.

For the performance data that you collect, and for the information that is available to your team members you need to consider how it meets each of the conditions:

◆ relevant to the specific purpose

◆ complete

◆ accurate

◆ timely

◆ in the right format

◆ at the right cost.

It is quite likely that the different team members will need different information, presented to suit their particular needs and formats. But you need to consider how you can meet their needs in a timely way and at a reasonable cost. For managers the challenge is to put in place systems that ensure formal and informal information can flow freely around the team, with no bottlenecks and blockages (human or technical) and be equally accessible to all who need it.

Finding the information you need

For many managers, their information needs are changing all the time, depending on the teams that they work with and the roles they fulfil. Managers need to be able to research and combine information from a range of sources to meet their needs, and also to share information effectively with others. As you read through this short case study, identify the types and sources of information that Chris is using.

When Chris was asked to research Project Management systems he started by using the Internet to identify possible suppliers and attended several software demonstrations. Although the demonstrations were impressive, Chris was sceptical about the manufacturer's claims – he had read in a trade journal that they were exaggerated. He also found it difficult to understand some of the technical jargon and desperately wanted a more practical insight and guidance on what he should do.

A colleague gave him details of a local company which had implemented a similar system. The co-ordinator there was able to give Chris a great deal of practical advice and to highlight the pitfalls. After a couple of visits, Chris felt much clearer about his requirements and asked four software suppliers to provide more detailed specifications and a quote.

After selecting the supplier, Chris negotiated a six week pilot to enable them to evaluate the software.

Chris is using information from a wide range of sources to help him develop his knowledge before he makes a decision. The information may be classified in a number of ways:

◆ Primary or secondary data. Primary data is original data collected in relation to the specific problem or decision whereas secondary data is data that has been previously collected for other purposes, generally by someone else. Trade journals, marketing literature and software demonstrations are all examples of secondary of data whereas the information that Chris has from site visits or from his supplier questionnaire or from the pilot was all primary (or original) data designed specifically to help Chris arrive at his decision.

◆ **Public or limited access.** Everyone can access the marketing literature on the websites but fewer people have access to the first hand experience of the local co-ordinator.

◆ **Hard or soft.** Is this information factual or is it based on opinion?

◆ **Formal or informal.** Formal information appears in reports, procedures and so on. Informal information comes from discussion with colleagues, your line manager, suppliers or customers, or through networking as in our case study.

◆ **Qualitative or quantitative.** Is it based on numbers or words? Is it enough to know that 'users were satisfied with the system', a qualitative statement, or do you need a quantitative statement like '90 per cent of users are satisfied'?

◆ **Internal or external.** Is the information created or available within the organisation, or do you have to access it through external sources such as journals or the Web?

Notice that one piece of information may fall into many categories. An email saying 'I think we have a problem with the cutting machine' provides internal, soft, qualitative, informal information.

The value of information

Primary (or original) data might be the most likely to give you an answer but there is a cost attached to it both in terms of time and money. Chris could, for example, have piloted a wider range of systems but it would have added both to his timescales and his budget. Also it's unlikely that the pilot will have given him all the information that he needed; long term performance for example. To provide a more complete picture and to save time and money, intelligence and research from secondary sources is often used by managers.

Look out for spin

Using secondary data is a cost effective approach but you do need to consider the source. Look quickly at the bar charts. What messages do they each give?

"There are three kinds of lies: lies, damned lies, and statistics."
Often attributed to Benjamin Disraeli

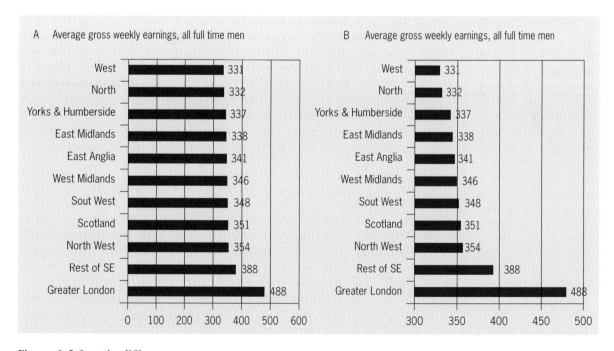

Figure 1.5 *Spot the difference*

Looking at them quickly can easily give very different messages. Chart B suggests that London pay is far greater than pay levels elsewhere – it would be useful for the manager in London trying to prevent a large pay rise. In contrast, chart A suggests that there is very little difference between pay levels.

It's a simple trick, involving omitting the origin from the horizontal scale in Chart B. It would not confuse anyone who looked at the charts carefully, but we do not look carefully at every piece of information. It is natural for people to present information that gives a least some 'spin' to the message.

Another point to consider is the extent to which the secondary information itself is based on pre-processed data? Consider the following example:

WonderProduct have increased their sales from 1.4% to 1.6% of the total market, in other words a change of

$$\frac{0.2 \times 100}{1.4} = 14\%$$

If corrected to one significant figure, the original figures become 1% and 2%, which show an increase of 100%. A trade journal that had only been supplied with those figures may correctly report the change as "WonderProduct claims to double output in year one".

By using pre-processed data the journal has exaggerated the actual growth by a factor of seven.

Think back to the earlier quotation from the Informix survey:

32% of the sample had made an important business decision in the past six months based on hope or luck.

You should now be starting to think about that statement more critically. How many managers were surveyed? How many managers replied to the survey request? In what industry, or culture, did those managers work?

Not knowing the answers to those, and other, questions, you cannot be sure how relevant the data is for you, or what conclusions you can draw.

Effective information sources need to be credible, unbiased and accurate. Generally speaking, the closer you can get to the original source of information, the more confident you can be in its accuracy. To evaluate your source, ask:

1. does the source have the necessary qualifications or levels of understanding to make the claim?

2. does the source have a reputation for accuracy?

3. does the source have a motive for being innacurate or biased?

4. does the source have the necessary data to support their claims?

Using the web

The biggest source of secondary data is now the World Wide Web and you need to be able to search it.

The starting point for all Web searches is a **search engine** – a tool that responds to an information request by searching the Web for what it interprets as relevant material. Search engines are also referred to as '**indexes**' as they act like gigantic indexes to selected chunks of the Web. They take an input search word (**search term**) or phrase, and retrieve a set of results (**hits**) that relate to that term or phrase from the Web pages that they have identified, collected into a virtual database and indexed. Note the word 'selected' – none of them scans absolutely everything, and you will need to learn which search engines are most useful for which purposes.

There are four basic types of search tool:

◆ free text search engines

◆ human-generated indexes

◆ metasearch tools

◆ natural language tools.

As search engines develop, the distinction between the types is becoming more blurred, and all types are continually improving.

Free-text search engines

Search engines retrieve a set of Web pages (hits) that match a word or phrase input by the user. They do not search the entire Web – only those pages that exist in the index of the search engine. The indexes are compiled by computer robots and can be vast. Google (www.google.com) and Alta Vista (www.altavista.com) are currently the biggest with billions of pages each. Since the indexing method is basically a free text search, the engine will retrieve every instance of the search term, whether it is relevant to your search or not. This means that if you're a bird enthusiast looking for information on 'cranes', you will also retrieve references to heavy lifting gear, maybe crane flies and companies that have crane in their title. On the other hand, these searches may not pick up useful **related terms**, so a search on 'boats' may not select references to 'yachts' or 'ships'.

19

Index-based search engines

Some companies also try to catalogue the Web. Whereas search engines use computers to create the search engine index, classified and specialist directories use humans to select and catalogue the Web pages. Yahoo (www.yahoo.com) is one of the most notable. As well as being able to enter search text, the user can also browse through the directory. For example, if you want to find a new movie, you might start with entertainment and then click movies and carry on until you find what you want.

There are numerous specialist directories that act as gateways to specific subjects on the Web. The medical gateway www.omni.ac.uk is an example. For a comprehensive list of what is available, go to www.vlib.org.

Metasearch engines

These are not search engines themselves – more tools that know about other search tools and will submit your query to several search engines at once. Metacrawler (www.metacrawler.com) and Dogpile (www.dogpile.com) are examples.

Natural-language search engines

Natural-language search engines are very appealing, as you can literally type in a question in the way that you would ask it. www.uk.Ask.com (previously AskJeeves) is one of the best known of these. Inputting: 'Who won the World Cup in 2006?' retrieves not only the result but details of many other World Cup and football-related sites.

Quantitative data from the Web

Since most enquiries to search engines are based on text, it is easy to conclude that the Web can provide qualitative, rather than quantitative, data and information. However, it is often very easy to find up-to-date, accurate quantitative data from reputable sources. We followed the process:

◆ Go to *Google* and use *More* to access the *Google Directory*

◆ Select *Business*, then *Mining and Drilling*, and then *Associations*

◆ Select *National Mining Association*

◆ Select *Statistics*

◆ Select *Facts about minerals*

◆ Select *Minerals Production. Mine Production Statistics of Selected Non-Fuel Minerals, 2000–2005*

◆ This gave data on the total U.S. mine production of 30 minerals for the five years 2000 to 2005.

To see what information is available, try a similar process in your own industry.

Getting better results

Choosing the right kind of search engine for your purpose will go a long way towards getting better search results more quickly.

A number of other techniques are available, including:

♦ using the terms AND, OR and NOT, or the operators + and – (e.g. car AND van to find sites with both words)

♦ putting phrases in quotes ('London Bridge' finds a specific structure; London Bridge will find all the bridges in London)

♦ criteria such as language, or expanded by the use of 'wildcard' characters.

Selected search engines

♦ Google (www.google.com)

♦ Alta Vista (www.altavista.com)

♦ Ask (previously Ask Jeeves) (www.uk.ask.com)

♦ Dogpile (www.dogpile.com)

♦ Excite (www.excite.com)

♦ HotBot (www.hotbot.com)

♦ Lycos (www.lycos.com)

♦ Metacrawler (www.metacrawler.com)

♦ Yahoo! (www.yahoo.com)

If you're looking for non-English language search engines, try www.searchenginecolossus.com which covers about 100 countries.

For suggestions on effective searching go to *Finding information: search engines* on www.philb.com/whichengine.htm

A list of useful sites can also be found on www.rba.co.uk/search/list.pdf

Privacy and Data Protection

If you work with information about people, you must be aware of their rights under Data Protection legislation. This concerns Personal Data – factual information or opinions that relate to a living individual (known as the Data Subject) and allows people to identify that individual. Personal Data may be as little as a name and address. The information can be held on a computer, CCTV system, taped telephone records or – provided the structure enables information about a specific individual to be found easily – in manual filing systems.

The legislation throughout Europe is based on eight principles, which can be summarised as follows:

The information itself	The information must be relevant, accurate and up-to-date.
	The data subject must give consent for collection and storage.
Using the information	The data subject must give consent for the specific use.
	The information must be protected if transferred outside the E.U.
Storing data	The information must be stored securely.
	Once the data is no longer needed it must be destroyed.
The data subject's rights	The data subject generally has a right to see the personal data.
	The data subject can prevent processing or use of data for direct marketing.

A key element of the legislation is the idea of 'consent'. As an example, employees who join a new organisation generally sign a form giving consent for the organisation to store data like names, addresses, pension and tax payments, and so on. On the other hand, employees do not give the organisation consent, for example, to sell their names and addresses to a direct mail company.

Activity 3
Finding relevant information

Objective

This activity will help you to find relevant information linked to your work, and also help you to select suitable sources and Web search engines in future.

Task

You have been asked to think about increasing the size of your team or department. You realise that, among other things, you will need to consider:

1 buying new equipment, perhaps from a manufacturer you have not used before.

2 the health and safety issues.

3 the trends in your industry, since you will be asked to justify the costs.

In each case, identify and comment on the effectiveness of internal and external sources of relevant information. In at least one case use a range of search engines, and techniques, and compare them so that you can use the most suitable engine/s in future.

	Internal sources		External sources	
	Source	Comments	Source	Comments
Industry trends				
Health and safety				
New equipment				

Search engine	Advantages	Disadvantages

Feedback

Future trends and predictions for your industry can be found in trade magazines or the journals of associations. You can probably also find them by searching the Web, following a process similar to the mining example we gave earlier.

General health and safety information is found in publicly available documents from the Health and Safety Executive (www.hse.gov.uk), or in documents from your own H&S department. Specific safety instructions from your organisation's H&S department may be issued as paper documents or over your organisation's computer network.

Trade prices of equipment used in your industry can often be found in trade magazines or the journals of associations. Retail prices may also be advertised or available in publicly available catalogues. Journals and catalogues may also be available over the Web. Your organisation may also have a direct internet link to the sales departments of a range of suppliers.

Table 1.2 summarises the key uses of some of the most common search engines.

Type of search engine	Example	What it's most useful for?
Free text search engines	Google.co.uk	When you know exactly what you want and can be specific about it. Good for 'Mercedes-Benz'; bad for 'performance cars'.
Index-based search engines	uk.yahoo.com directory.google.com	An overview of the subject area, structured so that you can narrow down a search or make it broader. For example, from 'Motor manufacturer' you can go up to the broader category 'Vehicle manufacturer' or down to the more specific 'Sports car manufacturer'.
Metasearch engines	dogpile.com	A broad and comprehensive view of sites in a subject area.
Natural language search	uk.ask.com	Good if you want a general look around a subject area.
Specialist indexes	omni.ac.uk	In-depth access to a highly specific subject area.

Table 1.2 *Key uses of the most common search engines*

Critical thinking

What goes wrong in decision making?

Even with information, decisions can still go badly wrong. Below we capture some of the factors that contribute to faulty decision making. Read through them and assess the extent to which any of them have affected your decision making in the past.

◆ **Selective use of data**. We are all tempted to give greater weight to data that supports our own case, and ignore those facts that disprove it. As an extreme example, think of the millions spent on research in the pharmaceutical industry – would you want to publish a report that showed that a new drug was not effective?

◆ **Premature termination of the search for evidence.** "We've got the evidence that supports our case. We don't need any more data."

◆ **Wishful thinking**, letting emotions make what should be a logical decision. "There's a 50% chance that it will work. I like the idea, let's try it."

◆ **Group think.** A group may focus more on consensus rather than on trying to find the best solution. This makes it very difficult for one person to say "I disagree. It won't work."

◆ **Personal biases and prejudice.** We each have personal biases and prejudices resulting from our unique life experiences which make it difficult to remain objective. For example if you believe that white vans are driven badly, then you'll notice whenever you see one speeding but tend to ignore all the other instances.

- **Incorrect assumptions.** For example It is rarely a safe assumption to say "Provided sales continue to rise...".

- **Circumstances may change** during the decision-making or implementation processes. During 2006 many estate agents trained their staff to carry out surveys for seller packs, not knowing that the government would change their plans.

- **Managers take an unrealistic view of what is achievable.** In December 2005, construction company Multiplex stated that Wembley would be ready for the May 2006 Cup Final. By August 2006, Multiplex said it was unlikely Wembley could hold a test event before June 2007.

Many of those difficulties can be avoided if the manager adopts a critical, or analytical, approach. Rather than trusting that things will turn out right, carefully follow a logical process and critically check your thoughts, actions and decisions at every stage.

The twelve key abilities of critical thinking are listed in Table 1.3. In the final column we've included questions relating to a company that wants to plan output levels for a number of different products.

Purpose	Key abilities		Typical comments
Clarification	1	Focusing on a question	Which product outputs are we considering?
	2	Analysing arguments	Why are we considering increasing production of Product B?
	3	Asking and answering questions of objectives and scope	Can we discuss closing output in our other factories?
	4	Defining terms, and judging definitions	Does 'Product B' include the other products that use Product B as a component?
	5	Identifying assumptions	What economies of scale are we assuming will result from doubling output?
Basic support	6	Judging the credibility of a source	Have Marketing correctly predicted sales levels in the past?
	7	Observing, and judging observation reports	They've based their predictions on the South East. Do we know anything about the North and Scotland?
	8	Deducing and judging deductions	Sales tend to follow the rules of supply and demand. I think the predicted increase in sales is realistic.
	9	Inducing, and judging inductions	When we increased output by 30% last time we doubled our profits. I'm not sure that we can assume it will happen again.
	10	Making and judging value judgements	I think the market is ready for a new product. But that's only a guess.
Strategic and tactical aspects	11	Deciding on an action	Based on all the information available, we should ...
	12	Interacting with others	I'm going to explain my suggestion. Tell me what you think and we can discuss it.

Table 1.3 *Critical thinking – the 12 key abilities*

Source: Adapted from Ennis (1987)

Activity 4
Critical thinking in practice

Objective

This activity will help you to understand how structured information systems are used for management decision making.

Task

1. Work through the list in *'What goes wrong with management decisions?'* and identify which of the factors, if any, have tended to affect your decision making in the past. What impact did this have on the quality of decision making? What might you do differently in a similar decision making situation in the future?

2. Focus on two or three decisions that you have recently been involved in. To what extent did the decision makers use the 12 key abilities shown in Table 1.3?

Feedback

As you worked through the factors that contribute to faulty decision making, you might have reflected on how effectively you use data and information to help you make decisions. Not all managers view data as essential for their effectiveness. Some tend to see data-driven decision making as mechanistic or boring and prefer to rely on their intuition and experience. Depending on training or personality, most people will favour either a rational or an intuitive approach.

As you thought about the people you work with, you might have identified different approaches. You can probably think of at least one person who works steadily to clarify the problem and evaluate the information until he or she can solve it and convince other people. You are also likely to have colleagues who have a very good feel for things or who jump quickly to decide a course of action and are very difficult to persuade even when the evidence suggests otherwise.

Although there is no doubting the value of intuitive judgments, the critical thinking abilities in Table 1.3 show that you need to go beyond intuition and the bounds of your own experience to become a critical thinker. Critical thinking involves acquiring information and being able to evaluate it objectively to reach a well justified conclusion.

Much does of course depend on the nature of the decision. There will be times when we need to make decisions without all the facts, often when time is imperative. In relation to many interpersonal questions, there might not even by any relevant factual information. Generally speaking however, opinions and decisions based on a critical analysis of the evidence stand on firmer ground than those formulated through less rational processes.

Knowing something of your natural decision making style and your biases can help you make the most of this book. If your natural tendency is to be intuitve, use this book to work out how you can use a more logical approach in future. If your preferred approach is to be rational, use this book to assess the effectiveness of your approach and to identify areas for improvement.

◆ Recap

Identify the information needs of your team and assess how effectively these are being met

◆ To manage information effectively you must define exactly what information you and your team needs. This will include information you need to achieve your objectives or to measure performance in your area.

◆ It is important to prioritise your information needs on the areas that really have an impact on performance and to ensure that the benefit of obtaining information outweighs the cost of obtaining it.

Consider the factors that affect the quality and use of data and information

◆ Data is unprocessed facts and figures without any added interpretation or analysis. Information is data that has been interpreted so that it has meaning for the user. Knowledge is a combination of information, experience and insight that may benefit the individual or the organisation.

◆ Data and information must be relevant to the specific purpose, complete, accurate, timely, in the right format, and available at a suitable price.

◆ Knowledge may be formal, explicit or generally available; or it may be instinctive, subconscious, tacit or hidden. We develop our own knowledge by analysing problems or situations.

Gather and record information relevant to your own area of responsibility, complying with any constraints on the collection of, and access to, data

◆ Sources of information may be internal or external; public or limited access; hard or soft; qualitative or quantitative; formal or informal. You need to take particular care when information has been processed for a purpose different from your own.

◆ The Web is a source of vast amounts of information, most easily accessed using suitable search engines and specific search techniques.

◆ If you work with information about people, you must be aware of their rights under Data Protection legislation. This generally applies to information from which the person could be identified. Data subjects must give consent for the specific use of the data, and generally have the right to see the personal data that you hold.

Explore the characteristics of critical thinking and assess your own critical thinking skills

◆ There are a number of reasons why management decisions go wrong, for example because they are based on incorrect assumptions, on insufficient information, or because situations change.

◆ Many of those difficulties can be avoided if the manager adopts a critical, or sceptical, approach. Carefully follow a logical process and critically check your thoughts, actions and decisions at every stage.

◆ The 12 abilities of critical thinking fall under three broad headings: clarification, basic support, and strategical and tactical aspects.

◆ Managers often have to make decisions based on insufficient information ('satisficing'). In these situations, it may be necessary to reconsider decisions as more information becomes available.

 More @

Bedward, D. and Stredwick, J. (2004) *Managing Information: Core Management,* **Elsevier**
This book provides an introduction to the use of information systems, finance and statistics.

Buckley, P. and Clark, D. (2004) *A Rough Guide to the Internet,* **Rough guides**
Written in plain English, this book covers everything from getting online for the first time to advanced tips and tricks.

McKenna, E.F. (1996) Business Psychology and Organisational Behaviour, Psychology Press
Chapter 5 of this book is titled Human Processing and Decision Making and discusses the different ways in which people make decisions.

Robson, W. (1997) *Strategic Management and Information Systems,* **Prentice Hall**
This describes the various types of management information system, and considers the information needs of managers from an Information Technology perspective.

Wilson, D. (2002) *Managing Information: IT for Business Process,* **Butterworth-Heinemann**
This book describes how successful organisations make best use of information and knowledge and explains why information technology is essential for the management of business processes.

Information Week (www.informationweek.com) and **Better Management** (www.bettermanagement.com) are both useful sites to search for downloadable articles, white papers and research reports.

2 Finding and showing the message in numbers

> **"Competitive advantage is gained by having sufficient people with the skills to analyse the growing flood of data, to present it convincingly and achieve the necessary improvements."**
> **David Wilson (2002)**

Data by itself rarely tells you much. To be told that oil is selling at $80 a barrel is meaningless unless you know something about typical prices over recent years and months, or how the barrel price translates into petrol prices at the pump. The person trading in oil will need to know about prices and trends over periods of hours and minutes. To create useful information, data must be used in context and must be presented clearly.

This theme starts with an overview of the various ways in which quantitative data can be presented. You will have met many of them before, but our aim here is to emphasise the advantages and disadvantages of each so that you can always select a suitable one for your purpose.

We then look at ways of analysing and interpreting the data to identify underlying trends or relationships.

Finally, you will need to explain your findings to other people. You may have to use your information to support your case or argument. The challenge here is to make the trends and relationships clear, without the audience thinking that you have oversimplified, or put a 'spin' on, the results.

Note that, throughout the theme we will use examples based on the small data sets, to ensure that the principles are clear. In practice, managers may have to deal with large data sets and use computer systems to make the calculations, but the basic principles of those calculations remain the same.

In this theme you will:

- compare how effectively various tables, charts and other visual tools present numeric data
- interpret raw data to aid understanding using tables, averages and frequency distributions
- select effective ways of presenting data to facilitate understanding and to support a case or argument.

Presenting data visually

The easiest way to present data is to tabulate it, but a diagram is usually a more effective way to communicate data because it's easier on the eye, particularly if there's a lot of data.

Tables

Study the simple example shown in Table 2.1.

	Output		
	2003	2004	2005
Product A	3,500	4,000	4,200
Product B	500	800	700
Product C	2,000	1,500	2,250
Total	6,000	6,300	7,150

Table 2.1 *Presenting data in a table*

Tables like this have a number of benefits:

◆ They can show a lot of detailed data.

◆ They can be used in many ways. For example, you could use the data to assess output of any of the products over the three years or to compare the output of each product in any one year.

On the other hand, there's one major problem. The user has to do quite a lot of work to get information from the data in this simple table, and the task of finding information gets harder as the number of rows and columns increases.

Few people could look at Table 2.1 and immediately identify trends or assess the relative importance of different products. For example, how long would it take you to identify which products had falls in sales in 2004 and 2005? And how long would you take to calculate what percentage of overall sales was achieved by product C in 2004?

However, it is often possible to present specific information more easily by analysing the data in the table. Tables 2.2 and 2.3 help you to quickly find the answers to the two questions above.

	Increase/decrease in sales on previous year	
	2004	2005
Product A	500	200
Product B	300	-100
Product C	-500	750
Total	300	850

Table 2.2 *Presenting information on sales trends*

	Percentage of overall sales		
	2003 (%)	2004 (%)	2005 (%)
Product A	59	63	59
Product B	8	13	10
Product C	33	24	31
Total	100	100	100

Table 2.3 *Presenting information on percentage of sales achieved by each product*

Table 2.2 quickly shows that Product C's sales fell during 2004, and Product A's sales fell during 2005. Table 2.3 immediately shows that Product B contributed the smallest percentage of overall sales in all three years.

Manipulating data in this way can present information more clearly. Unfortunately, every time you try to clarify the information, you are likely to lose some of the original data. For example neither of the later tables shows the actual sales levels.

The various charts and diagrams that we'll now describe all aim to make things easier for the user. They aim to clarify the data and create useful information. As you saw with tables, however, in clarifying the information charts often lose some of the original data. For each of the charts and diagrams, try to identify their particular benefits and disadvantages for your own work.

Pie charts

Pie charts are among the most common tools for clarifying data. The slices of the pie are drawn so the angles represent the size of each component. For example, the first of the pie charts in Figure 2.1 (for 2003) shows that output of Product A is 59 per cent of the total output.

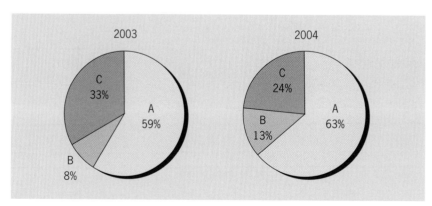

Figure 2.1 *Simple pie charts showing product output 2003 and 2004*

A single pie chart shows two factors very easily:

1. It allows quick comparison of the components. For example, in the 2003 chart it's immediately obvious that the number of Product A is about twice the number of Product C.

2. Comparing two pie charts can show how the importance of one component has changed. For example the slice of pie for Product B increased between 2003 and 2004.

On the other hand, pie charts do not give clear information where there is a large number of similarly-sized components. Think what the pie charts would look like if the company sold 15 products.

There is also one major problem when comparing two pie charts. If the two pies are the same size, many users will assume that the total output of all three products is the same in 2003 and 2004. The pie charts don't actually give any information about total output, they only show proportions, but users can easily get the wrong message.

Creating impressive charts

Software like Microsoft® Excel can create charts that are visually more impressive or effective, for example like the 'exploded' three-dimensional pie chart shown in Figure 2.2, but notice that this doesn't give any more information than a simple pie chart.

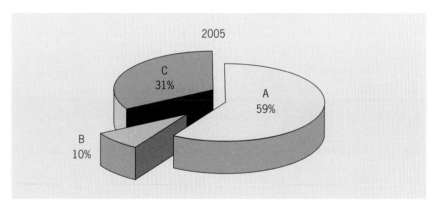

Figure 2.2 *Exploded pie chart showing product output 2005*

Bar chart

Bar charts are more effective than pie charts at showing actual values. For example, look at Figure 2.3, which shows the 2004 product output.

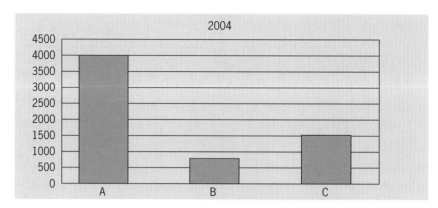

Figure 2.3 *Basic bar chart showing product output 2004*

This very clearly shows the actual output of the three products during 2004. On the other hand, it's less effective at showing how many times greater the output of Product A is than the output of Product B.

A wide range of types of bar chart are available. As with pie charts and basic bar charts, they can each clarify particular types of data, but are less effective at other tasks.

Look at the two more complex types of bar chart in Figures 2.4 and 2.5, which have been compiled using the product data from our earlier examples. In each case they clarify some aspects of the data well, but they show other things less well.

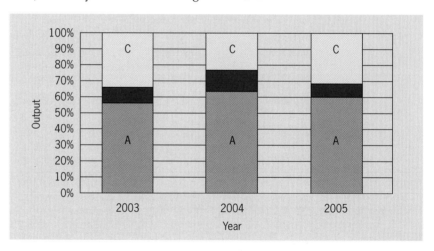

Figure 2.4 *Stacked bar chart*

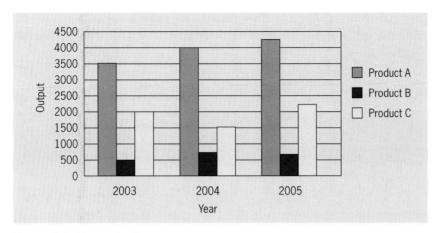

Figure 2.5 *Clustered columns*

Figure 2.4 works rather like a pie chart. It shows the relative importance of each product very well, but is less good at showing how each product's sales change from year to year. It also can give a false message that overall sales stay constant.

Figure 2.5 clearly shows the relative importance of each product. It also gives a clear message about how Product A changes, but is less clear about Products B and C.

Line graphs

So far we've drawn charts that relate to groups, for example the group of products created in 2003. Now we need to look at charts that show gradual changes or trends. Line graphs are used to analyse measurements over time or some other dimension, in this case the variation in thickness of a metal beam over its length.

The line graph in Figure 2.6 shows measurements of the thickness of a metal beam, taken at metre intervals.

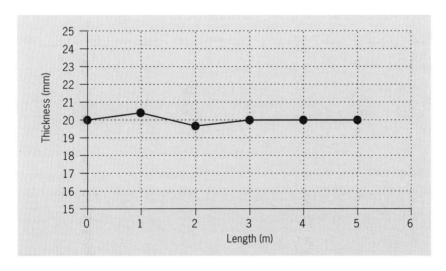

Figure 2.6 *Line graph showing thickness of metal beam at 1 metre intervals*

If the specification is that the thickness must be between 19 mm and 21 mm, then this beam seems to be within specification. But what happens if we take measurements at smaller intervals? Using measurements taken at 0.1m intervals, we get the results shown in Figure 2.7.

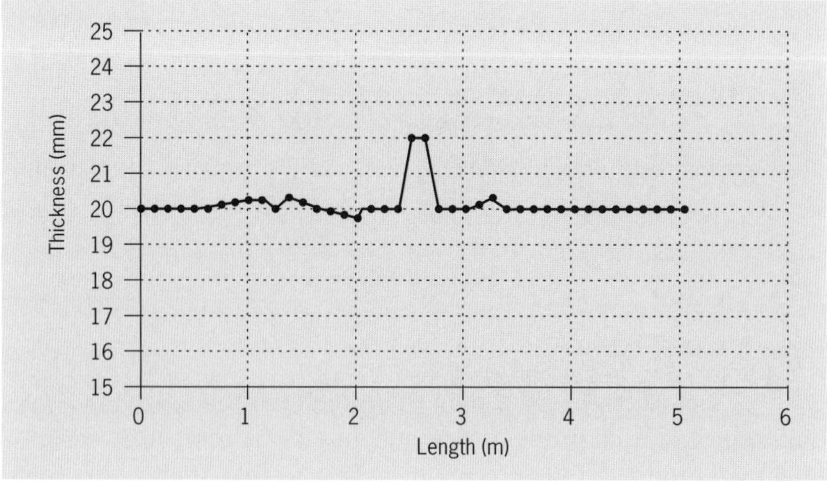

Figure 2.7 *Line graph showing thickness of metal beam at 0.1 metre intervals*

This shows a large increase in thickness at about 2.6 m. There's a 'lump' on the beam which wasn't picked up by the first set of measurements. The beam is not within the specification of between 19 mm and 21 mm thick. Using an appropriate scale that will make the points visible on the graph is crucial if the line graph to be useful as an analytical tool.

Inconsistencies in measurements (as in this example) or trends over time are the two most common observations from a line graph. However, you must not assume that there is a gradual change between each of the points on the chart (compare the shape of the two graphs between the 2 m and 3 m measurements).

Activity 5
Presenting data

Objective

This activity will help you to compare how effectively various tables, charts and other visual tools present data, and help you to select suitable tools in future.

Task

A team of sales staff send in their records each month. These are recorded on a spreadsheet. How would you present that data most clearly for the following situations? In each case identify any potential problems or disadvantages of choosing that method.

a) To record the raw data.

b) To show total sales by the team in each month of the past year.

c) To show trends in the total sales by the team in each month of the past year.

d) To identify the 'above-average' members of the team.

e) To identify any team members whose performance is improving.

Feedback

Feedback to this activity is provided on page 48.

Interpreting raw data

Approaches to presenting data may be very basic – simply organising the data so that it is easy to use. An example of this approach is Table 2.13, where the data on individual sales is presented in alphabetical order. Or the approach may involve interpreting the data – looking at it in different ways to see what it shows. Table 2.14 highlights the above average performers, and Figure 2.12 makes it easy to identify downward trends in individual performance.

Interpretation is about using the data to increase your understanding.

Tables

Within tables, you've already seen how techniques like totalling and highlighting can be used. As a further example, consider the data in Table 2.4, showing the measurement of the weight of a certain product.

Sample	A	B	C	D	E	F	G
Weight (kg)	10.0	10.2	10.8	10.3	10.3	10.4	10.5

Table 2.4 *Weights of product samples*

If the product specification gives a weight range of 10.0 to 10.5 kg, then this table could be re-written to highlight any out-of-specification samples, see Table 2.5.

Sample	A	B	C	D	E	F	G
Weight (kg)	-	-	10.8	-	-	-	-

Table 2.5 *Weights of out-of-specification samples*

Table 2.5 clearly identifies the over-weight sample. However, it has lost what might be important information. Looking again at Table 2.4, and ignoring Sample C, shows that the weight of the sample is gradually rising. This information is not shown in Table 2.5.

The question of significant figures involves a similar task of clearly identifying why you are using the data. Table 2.6 shows more significant figures, but adds absolutely nothing useful if you want to know which samples are out of specification.

Sample	A	B	C	D	E	F	G
Weight (kg)	10.012	10.223	10.824	10.364	10.354	10.432	10.523

Table 2.6 *Weights of product samples (5 sig. fig.)*

In contrast, Table 2.7 shows the data with fewer significant figures. It's very easy to read, but it actually changes the apparent quality of sample G. It now seems as if Sample G is out of specification.

Sample	A	B	C	D	E	F	G
Weight (kg)	10	10	11	10	10	10	11

Table 2.7 *Weights of product samples (2 sig. fig.)*

These examples highlight the need to balance two factors. When interpreting data you want to identify and present a clear message, but each time you simplify the data there is a risk that you will lose key information and accuracy.

Summarising data using averages

> Then there was the man who drowned crossing a stream with an average depth of six inches.
> **W. I. E. Gates**

There are various averages that you can use to summarise or describe a set of data, but they need to be used carefully or they can be quite misleading, as shown in the following case study.

The owner of the small company EarnMoney plc is paid £60,000 per year. There are nine workers; four are paid £21,000 per year and five are paid £15,000. What is the average pay?

If you add the total wage bill and divide by the total number of employees, you'll get what is called the **mean**. This gives:

$$\text{mean} = \frac{60{,}000 + (4 \times 21{,}000) + (5 \times 15{,}000)}{10}$$

$$= £21{,}900$$

This figure would be really useful if the managing director wanted to show how well the workers are paid. It also gives useful information about the total amount spent on wages. It doesn't, however, give a completely accurate picture – nobody except the managing director actually earns more than £21,000.

To show what the most typical pay rate, we use the **mode**. The mode shows the most common of the figures, which in our example would be £15,000. Again, this doesn't give a particularly accurate picture – the most common figure is also the lowest rate.

Finally, you can write each of the figures in order and choose the middle one (the **median**). Writing each person's pay (and missing out the thousands) we get:

15, 15, 15, 15, **15**, **21**, 21, 21, 21, 60

With ten numbers we get two 'middle ones', which we have highlighted. Calculating the mean of those two figures gives us:

$$\frac{15 + 21}{2} = 18$$

So, the median pay is also £18,000.

The three types of average can be used both to clarify and to mislead (or 'spin' the data). It is accurate to say "The most common pay rate is £15,000", or "Half the people get paid under £18,000", but both statements hide the fact that quite a lot of employees actually get £21,000. It is accurate to say that "The 10 people get paid £219,000", but that hides the fact that the managing director gets almost three times as much as anyone else.

Think about how the three types of average are used in your own work. Does their use clarify the information or does it confuse people? Would it help if the word 'average' was replaced by the terms mean, mode and median?

Frequency distributions

In some analyses, you will collect a lot of data. How can you use this data and make it meaningful?

Imagine you are asked by your manager to collect information on how the business uses office space. You start by collecting data on how many people work in each office throughout the building. The raw data is:

1, 3, 3, 4, 3, 3, 6, 1, 2, 3, 2, 2, 5, 3, 4, 2, 3, 5, 4, 3.

Frequency tables (Table 2.8) are one option for presenting this data. Frequency means the number of times that a value occurs.

Number of workers	Frequency
1	2
2	4
3	8
4	3
5	2
6	1
Total	20

Table 2.8 *Frequency of office size*

Note that, in making this table, some detail has been lost immediately. You have no way of knowing that there is a one person office next door to the six person office.

On the other hand there has been a gain in clarity. The table immediately shows that 3-person office is the most common.

The information can also be presented as a **histogram**, as shown in Figure 2.8.

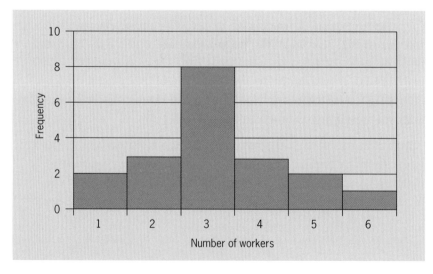

Figure 2.8 *Histogram showing numbers of workers per office*

The histogram very clearly shows the maximum value and the range of values. On the other hand it would not work well if the range of workers in the offices varied from, say, 1 to 60.

Grouped data

Histograms work as long as the number of possible data values is not too great to be able to draw the graph. Above 10 values, the table and histogram can become as confusing to read as the original data. When this happens, the data must be grouped.

As an example of **grouped data**, consider a machine which weighs products to the nearest gram, for example producing readings of 1103, 1110, 1019, 992, 983 and so on. A chart showing each value to the nearest gram would be meaningless unless the number of products was extremely large, and it would then be extremely tedious to collect the data and present it.

In practice the values would be grouped, for example as shown in Table 2.9.

Weight (gm)	Frequency
941-960	20
961-980	37
981-1000	350
1001-1020	323
1021-1040	80
1041-1060	10

Table 2.9 *Grouped data*

This then makes it easy to present as a histogram, as shown in Figure 2.9.

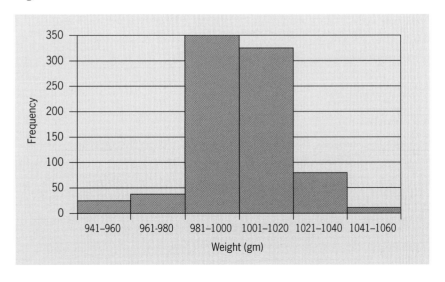

Figure 2.9 *Grouped data shown in a histogram*

41

In many situations, the actual number in each column is relatively unimportant. It is more relevant to show the data as a percentage of the overall total, for example stating that the number of products in the range 1001 to 1020 gm is 34.2%. This can be shown as a **frequency distribution**, see Figure 2.10.

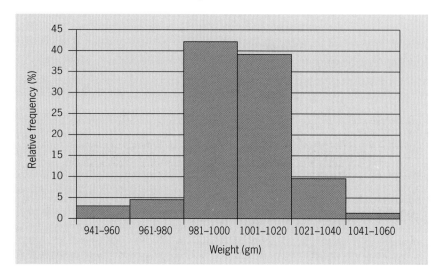

Figure 2.10 *A frequency distribution*

Notice that the title and the scale on the vertical axis have changed, but there has been no change to the basic shape of the chart.

Presenting discrete and continuous data

In the earlier examples in this section we have considered data which can have only have certain stated values, such as the number of people who work in an office. An office might be occupied by two or three people, but not by 2.5 people. This type of data is known as **discrete data**; it changes in a series of steps.

Many other forms of data can have a much wider range of values. A weight can in fact be measured to almost any degree of precision that we want, for example 1090.134565296 gm. A person's age is another example. Data which changes gradually is known as **continuous data**.

Frequency tables and histograms can be used to represent both discrete and continuous data, but the data must be treated slightly differently:

◆ Frequency tables. A frequency table for discrete data states the actual numbers represented (e.g. 6-workers) but for continuous data can only represent a range of values (e.g. a volume of more than 64 ml but less than 65 ml).

◆ Histograms. One column of a histogram for discrete data represents a specific value (6-workers) or a specific range (1041-1060 gm). The value or the range are shown on the histogram. In contrast a histogram for continuous data shows the mid-point of each column and implies a range of possible values.

For example a column marked 67 would represent all values from 66.5 to 67.4.

As the number of data sets increases, then it becomes possible to use more sophisticated statistical tools such as standard deviation to analyse the data. You look further at this in the later theme on Analytical Statistics.

Activity 6
Interpreting data

Objective

This activity will help you to assess the benefits and disadvantages of using tables, averages and frequency distributions to interpret raw data.

Task

1. As Health and Safety Director for a multinational company you have access to data on accidents throughout the organisation. You are currently focusing on two tasks:

   a) Preparing a summary for the Board, showing the past year's performance in relation to Health and Safety.

   b) Preparing for a meeting with the H&S managers from each region.

   You have reduced the amount of data to a spreadsheet showing total monthly accident rates in each region, and corresponding figures for the past four years.

   You also have access to data on:

   ◆ the number of branches in each region and the total numbers of employees

   ◆ data on typical and best practice results for H&S in your industry.

   How would you interpret the data and plan to present it at the two meetings?

2. Think of two contrasting meetings that you will be involved in the near future. What information do you have available at present? How could you interpret that data to identify any trends or issues? How would you present that data to explain the situation to other people?

Feedback

1. a) The Board will be looking primarily for an overview, but may also want to explore the situation more closely. After getting an overview, the two key questions are likely to be about trends (e.g. whether accident rates are improving), and whether there are significant differences between different regions.

   A good starting place will be to calculate the total number of accidents for the whole organisation. This could be presented as a histogram showing how that performance compares with best practice and industry average figures.

   To analyse trends, you should consider both the whole organisation and the individual regions. The clearest approach is probably to draw one line graph showing total accidents over the last five years, and then another showing trends for each region. Note that, if the number of employees in a region has changed, you will need to calculate the number of accidents per employee rather than using the number of accidents per region.

   When comparing the number of accidents per region you will almost certainly have to consider the number of employees. On the other hand, if the high-risk work only involves, say, five employees in each branch you may instead need to calculate the number of accidents per branch.

   b) When meeting with regional H&S managers, you could begin with an overview based on the information presented to the Board. However, the main focus must then turn to each of the regions.

   You will certainly want to compare current regional performance on the basis of both the number of employees and the number of branches. Comparing these figures may, for example, identify that there are more accidents per employee in regions where there is a large number of small branches.

   You will also want to do some preparatory investigation relating to the types of accident. For example is the number of manual lifting accidents per employee higher in certain regions?

2. Thinking of your future meetings, the key tasks are to:
   - collect all the relevant information
   - use some of the techniques described above to identify the trends and issues that you can predict or expect
   - use different techniques to try to identify trends or issues that are not immediately obvious
   - use a variety of presentional techniques to clearly demonstrate the trends and issues.

Presenting your case

This theme has focused on the need to use analytical techniques to interpret data and create useful information. It has emphasised the benefits of showing information clearly and accurately, so that you can persuade other people that your arguments or conclusions are valid and will create benefits. Managers who are critical thinkers are good at using information to frame and present their own arguments.

In this final section we will look in a little more detail at two key issues relating to presentation:

◆ Explaining your approach – taking the reader step-by-step through your argument.

◆ Accuracy and clarity – how can you balance the need to present a clear message while at the same time convincing your audience that the data is accurate and relevant?

Explaining your approach

If people are to accept your argument, it must be both logical and persuasive. Stephen Toulmin, an English philosopher and logician, identified three elements of a persuasive argument:

◆ The *conclusion* of the argument that you are asking the other person to accept.

> The 22% drop in production was caused by faults on production line 2. We need to enhance the skills of our maintenance team to support the line.

◆ The *facts* and *evidence* that support the conclusion. These should be indisputable.

> Production line 2 was out of action for three weeks. The maintenance engineer with responsibility for Line 2 was off sick for that time.

◆ The *warrant* or the bridge between your conclusion and the evidence. This is where you describe how you have used the evidence to arrive at your conclusion.

Production line 2 contributes 30% of total production capacity. The manufacturer no longer supports the technology in the UK and parts have to be ordered from China and fitted by our own maintenance staff. Only one of the engineers has the specialist knowledge necessary He was off sick last month. The two other engineers are fully competent on the two newer lines and could be coached by our specialist engineer on the workings of production line 2.

Accuracy and clarity

"It's hard to argue with apparent facts even if you suspect that they are wrong "
Charles Handy, Understanding organisations

Two of the most common ways of increasing clarity are to reduce the number of significant figures in the data, or to summarise the data set, for example by showing the average income of 4 quarters rather than over 12 months. In many situations these techniques are very useful, but there is always a risk that valuable information will be lost, as shown in the three sections of Table 2.10.

A	Month	J	F	M	A	M	J	J	A	S	O	N	D
	Value	13.5	14.5	15.5	15.5	14.5	13.5	13.5	14.5	15.5	15.5	14.5	15.5
B	Quarters	1	2	3	4								
	Average value (3 s.f.)	14.5	14.5	14.5	15.2								
C	Quarters	1	2	3	4								
	Average value (2 s.f.)	15	15	15	15								

Table 2.10 *Tables that 'clarify' the data*

A shows the raw data. In an attempt to present clear information, the values are averaged over quarterly periods in B – the values completely lose the six month cyclic variations of the raw data.

In C, the attempt to clarify the information by reducing the number of significant figures suggests that values are constant throughout the year, quite a contrast to the raw data shown in A.

These examples are, of course, extreme, but they do suggest a general rule – whenever you try to simplify raw data there is a risk that something important will be lost. The risk becomes greater every time the same data is 're-clarified'.

Activity 7
Presenting your case

Objective

This activity will help you to select effective ways of presenting data to facilitate understanding and to support a case or argument.

Task

Table 2.11 shows data on a national mining industry for the period 1990 to 2005.

Year	90	91	92	93	94	95	96	97	98	99	00	01	02	03	04	05
Number of mines	4335	4025	3703	3429	3268	2946	2689	2609	2493	2306	2124	2144	2065	1972	2011	1982
Production (million tonnes)	1001	1050	1046	1010	1020	1025	1030	1074	1100	1124	1145	1180	1156	1050	1067	1091
Number of inspectors	810	847	830	770	725	665	590	610	645	646	656	605	622	620	594	584
Number of serious accidents	6680	6232	5567	4785	4573	4756	3967	3025	2935	3546	3856	4289	2745	3025	2876	2341

Table 2.11 *Mining safety statistics 1990–2005*

a) What trends can you identify from those figures?

b) What conclusion/s can you draw?

c) How would you demonstrate those trends to a meeting?

d) Which issue/s need further investigation?

Feedback

You could investigate these figures using a spreadsheet to calculate, for example, accidents per tonne produced, or accident per mine. Alternatively, you could draw histograms or line graphs.

a) Among the trends you could identify are the following:

♦ A gradual decrease in the number of mines.

♦ A gradual decrease in the number of accidents and inspectors, apart from a small rise in both between 1997 and 2001.

♦ A relatively constant level of overall production, though there was a significant increase between 1997 and 2001.

b) Some possible conclusions are:

- average output from mines increased

- larger mines have fewer accidents per tonne of output

- having larger mines means that fewer inspectors are needed per tonne of national output.

c) The trends could be shown as histograms or line graphs. Since there are 15 data sets, it is probably clearer to use line graphs. Since there are only four variables, they could all be shown in the same chart – this would clearly show the link between output, accidents and inspectors in the years 1997 to 2001. Note that you could use a different scale for inspector numbers, showing this on the right hand axis of the chart.

d) The key issue in these figures is the rise in accidents in 1997 to 2001. Was it caused by the rise in output, or was there some other cause? Further investigation is needed, if the industry is to avoid a further rise in accidents in future.

Feedback for Activity 5

1a) and b)

The raw data can be recorded in a simple table, and total sales can be shown as the sums of each column. These two sets of data are shown in Table 2.12.

Note some factors that make the table easy to use, for example column headings, units, and entries in alphabetical order.

	Monthly sales (£'000)					
	Jan	Feb	Mar	Apr	May	June
Andy	30	35	30	45	40	35
Beth	20	40	30	30	35	25
Carl	50	50	45	40	35	30
Diana	50	45	45	40	45	50
Ed	30	35	40	40	30	35
Total sales	180	205	190	195	185	175

Table 2.12 *Monthly sales (individuals and totals)*

c) Trends are most easily shown in a bar chart, see Figure 2.11. The main disadvantage is that it is harder for a user to identify the exact level of sales in each month.

Note that, if we had used a line graph it would have incorrectly suggested that, for example, sales gradually rose during January from £180K to £205.

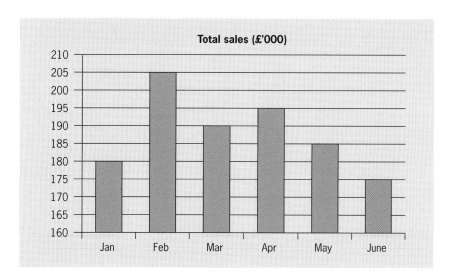

Figure 2.11 *Total monthly sales*

d) Table 2.13 shows one way of identifying the above-average sales staff. The last row shows the average sales per month. The individual sales rates that are above the average are shown in blue for each month. It demonstrates quickly that only Diana achieved above average results each month.

	Jan	Feb	Mar	Apr	May	June
Andy	30	35	30	45	40	35
Beth	20	40	30	30	35	25
Carl	50	50	45	40	35	30
Diana	50	45	45	40	45	50
Ed	30	35	40	40	30	35
Average monthly sales	36	41	38	39	37	35

Table 2.13 *Performance compared with average rates*

e) To compare the trends of each person's sales we drew a series of line graphs. To show the results clearly without using many colours, we have only included three sets of data. Table 2.13 quickly shows that Carl's results are gradually declining.

Note that this approach would not work for large number of sale staff, or where each person's levels of sales were very similar.

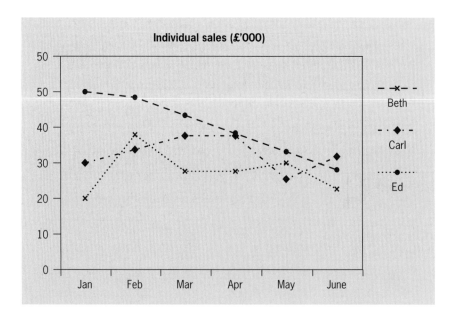

Figure 2.12 *Trends in individual sales*

Conclusion

Note that the aim of this activity is not primarily to assess which presentation method work best for sales records. It is to emphasise that different methods must be used, carefully selected to suit the needs of the various people who will study the information.

Completing part (2) of the activity should help you to look at presentation from the user's viewpoint. The method used must clearly and accurately give the information needed, without causing confusion or information overload.

◆ Recap

Compare how effectively various tables, charts and other visual tools present data

- Tables can show a lot of detailed data and can be used to present that data in many ways. But users have to work to get information from the data and the task gets harder as the number of rows and columns increases.

- Every time you clarify information, you risk losing some of the original data.

- Pie charts allow quick comparison of the relative importance of each component, provided the number of components is small.

- Bar charts allow quick comparison between different components and can show actual values. Each type of complex bar chart offers specific benefits.

◆ Line graphs usefully demonstrate measurements and trends over a distance or a period of time. You must not assume that there is a gradual change between each of the points on the chart.

Interpret raw data to aid understanding using tables, averages and frequency distributions

◆ Techniques like totalling, averaging and highlighting can be used to interpret data in tables. Care is needed to ensure that the clear message accurately reflects the original data.

◆ The three kinds of average (mean, mode and median) each give specific information. The mean is the total value divided by the number of elements; the mode is the value of the most common element; and the median is the value of the middle element.

◆ Frequency tables and histograms show, for example, how many examples there are in each data set. Where there are large numbers of possible data values, the data is grouped and shown as a frequency distribution.

◆ Where sufficient data is available you can use more sophisticated statistical tools such as those described later in this book.

Select effective ways of presenting data to facilitate understanding and to support a case or argument

◆ Clarity must be balanced against the need for accuracy and clarity. You need to present a clear message while at the same time convincing your audience that the data is accurate and relevant.

◆ Spin is inevitable. Every time you select a method of presentation you are, consciously or unconsciously, emphasising certain aspects of the information.

◆ Logical flow is essential if people are to follow your argument. The information must be presented in a series of logical steps based on accurate information.

▶▶ More @

- ◆ The Wikipedia website contains a good summary of the various visual tools and links to a number of other sites, including some open-source software that you can experiment with. See:

  http://en.wikipedia.org/wiki/Gantt_chart
  http://en.wikipedia.org/wiki/Ishikawa_diagram
  http://en.wikipedia.org/wiki/Flowcharts

  You will find other useful guidance on various websites by searching for the relevant visual tool.

- ◆ **Dretke, B.J. (2001)** *Statistics with Microsoft® Excel* **Prentice Hall** is a very useful guide to using a spreadsheet to create tables and charts and to make standard statistical calculations, for example using σ and Z-scores.

- ◆ Three useful textbooks on the practical uses of statistics are:

  - **Owen, F. and Jones, R. (1994)** *Statistics*, **Pitman**

  - **Wisniewski, M. (1997)** *Quantitative Methods for Decision Makers*, **Pitman**

  - **Buglear, J. (2005)** *Quantitative Methods for Business: The A-Z of QM*, **Elsevier**

3 Using computer tools

The development of computers since the introduction of the PC in 1980 has completely changed the way in which we analyse and present data. Software can help you to find the message in data. There are specialist statistical packages but for most business analyses spreadsheets provide the functionality that you need. Spreadsheets are excellent for preparing documents that consist mainly of numbers. They are fairly straightforward to use for both calculations and for the drawing of charts and diagrams.

> "Students today depend too much upon ink. They don't know how to use a pen knife to sharpen a pencil. Pen and ink will never replace the pencil."
> **National Association of Teachers, 1907**

On the other hand, computer tools can only carry out specific tasks, following exactly the procedure that they have been set. They have no intuitive feel for the data. As an example, consider the problem of finding the mean of three prices £19.00, £20.00, and £2100. A person would query whether the final figure was correct (should it be £21.00?). A computer will give the answer £713. As you work through this theme, never forget the importance of the accuracy of the original data. Remember the mnemonic GIGO – Garbage In, Garbage Out.

In this theme you will assess the use, benefits and limitations of spreadsheets to analyse and present qualitative data.

Spreadsheets

We'll begin this discussion of spreadsheets by looking at three questions. First, how can spreadsheets help you to present data clearly in tables? Second, what functions are available to analyse and process the data? And finally, how can spreadsheets be used to perform 'what if' calculations that assess the effect of changing one or more of the variables in a situation.

We look also at how you can use spreadsheets to create tables and graphs.

Entering and presenting data

You will have been told many rules about presenting information in spreadsheets, most of them designed to make it easy for users to find the information they want. Have a look at Table 3.1 and ask how effectively it gives you the information that you might need.

Name of product	Cost	Selling price	%
Alpha	20	25	0.25
Beta	15	20	0.33333
Gamma	10	15 (this season only)	0.5

Table 3.1 *A confusing table*

The table is difficult to use for at least five reasons:

1. The heading for the % column is unclear – what do the values show?

2. There are no units for the cost or selling price (are they measured in £, p, € or $?)

3. The additional information about the selling price of Gamma makes it difficult to compare the various values in that column – it should be in a footnote.

4. The figures in the cost column are not aligned, again making them difficult to compare.

5. The number of decimal places in the % column is inconsistent. This makes it difficult to compare them. There is also a question of exactly what the figures mean – remember that 0.5 means any number in the range 0.45 to 0.55, but 0.50 means any number in the range 0.495 to 0.505.

Even assuming that the spreadsheet is effective on the screen, you then need to think about how people will use it in practice. If they are likely to print it off, will they use a colour printer? If they will not, then the effect of any colour that you use to highlight specific data will be lost. If the table contains many columns, but few rows, should you set the page setup so that is prints in landscape rather than portrait mode?

When entering the data, how will you identify errors such as misplaced decimal points or sets of data put in the wrong column? How will you update the data – can you use version numbers to show that new data was added in September 2006?

Using functions

As an example of the uses of a simple function, look at Tables 3.2 to 3.4.

First name	Surname	Age	Home town	Annual pay
		Yrs		£
Paul	Baker	18	Midtown	12,000
Peter	Andrews	21	Newton	15,500
Margaret	Jones	25	Oldville	17,000
Gary	Peters	53	Oldville	21,000
Bhati	Patel	32	Oldville	19,000
Jane	Marshall	47	Midtown	20,000
Andy	Smith	20	Newton	16,000

Table 3.2 *Work team data*

First name	Surname	Age	Home town	Annual pay
		yrs		£
Paul	Baker	18	Midtown	12,000
Jane	Marshall	47	Midtown	20,000
Andy	Smith	20	Newton	16,000
Peter	Andrews	21	Newton	15,500
Margaret	Jones	25	Oldville	17,000
Bhati	Patel	32	Oldville	19,000
Gary	Peters	53	Oldville	21,000

Table 3.3 *Work team data – sorted by home town*

First name	Surname	Age	Home town	Annual pay
		yrs		£
Paul	Baker	18	Midtown	12,000
Peter	Andrews	21	Newton	15,500
Andy	Smith	20	Newton	16,000
Margaret	Jones	25	Oldville	17,000
Bhati	Patel	32	Oldville	19,000
Jane	Marshall	47	Midtown	20,000
Gary	Peters	53	Oldville	21,000

Table 3.4 *Work team – sorted by annual pay*

Table 3.2 shows the raw data as it was entered into the spreadsheet. Table 3.3 shows the data sorted according to where the team members live – a useful approach if you were planning a bus system to collect people for work. Table 3.4 shows the data sorted according the pay level – the approach you might use if you were assessing the effect of possible pay rise.

The function *Sort* that was used to create these tables is clearly a very useful tool, yet it only takes a very few key-strokes. For example to create Table 3.4 from Table 3.3 using Microsoft Excel you would select *Sort* from the *Data* menu, select *Column* and *Ascending* or *Descending*, and click *OK*.

The list of functions available in commercially popular spreadsheet packages is far greater than any manager will ever need. The challenge is to find the ones that are useful for yourself. Consider just a few examples that might be useful when assessing the quality of the output from a production machine. In relation to the length of a sample of items you might use the following functions:

◆ AVERAGE gives the mean value of the lengths

◆ CONVERT converts the data to a different system of measurement (perhaps from centimetres to inches)

◆ COUNT tells you how many items have been measured

◆ MAX gives the length of the largest item

◆ MODE gives the most commonly occurring length

◆ PERCENTILE tells you how many items were, for example, within the top 5% of the range.

What-if? calculations

One particularly useful use of functions is to carry out What-if? calculations. Look at the values and functions in Table 3.5. For example, what would be the impact if the current operating costs for wages, materials and heating rose by x%.

A/1	B	C	D	E
2	Inputs	Current cost (£k)	Predicted rise (%)	Estimated cost (£k)
3	Wages	50	X	=B2*(100+X)/100
4	Materials	40	Y	=C2*(100+Y)/100
5	Heating	30	Z	=D2*(100+Z)/100
6	Total	=sum(C3:C5)		=sum(E3:E5)

Table 3.5 *Planning a What-if? calculation*

The table is designed so that the values that appear in column E depend on the values inserted into column D. For example inserting equal values of 5% for every predicted rise gives estimated costs as shown in Table 3.6. In contrast, Table 3.7 shows that a large increase in heating costs cannot be completely overcome by limiting wage increases to 3%.

A/1	B	C	D	E
2	Inputs	Current cost (£k)	Predicted rise (%)	Estimated cost (£k)
3	Wages	50	5	52.5
4	Materials	40	5	42.0
5	Heating	30	5	31.5
6	Total	120		126.0

Table 3.6 *What if the predicted rises were all 5%?*

A/1	B	C	D	E
2	Inputs	Current cost (£k)	Predicted rise (%)	Estimated cost (£k)
3	Wages	50	3	51.5
4	Materials	40	5	42.0
5	Heating	30	10	33.0
6	Total	120		126.5

Table 3.7 *Can wages be controlled to overcome an increase in heating costs?*

Using spreadsheets to create charts

Charts and graphs are highly effective spreadsheet tools that can be used during the analysis of data and also to present information clearly. The graphical formats that we looked at in the previous theme can be explored easily.

Consider Figure 3.1, two histograms for two telephone operators showing how long they took to respond to a number of calls. The vertical dotted line shows the target specification.

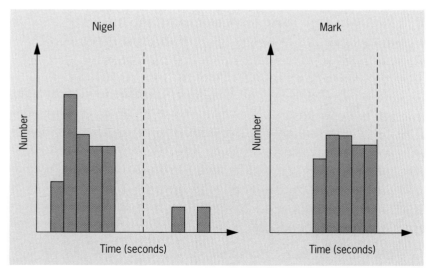

Figure 3.1 *Performance of two telephone operators*

The raw data showing the time to answer each call would be quite difficult to interpret, though you could probably identify the instances where Nigel took a long time to respond. The mean average for the two operators would be roughly the same. Yet drawing the charts shows that the two operators actually perform very differently. Nigel usually answers the phone more quickly, but sometimes is very slow – Mark is slower on average, but more consistent. As their manager you would take quite different approaches when trying to improve each person's performance.

That case shows an example of how drawing a chart can identify a problem or situation that you might not otherwise notice. We now need to look at the key factors that you must consider when presenting charts to an audience.

Creating persuasive charts – the key factors

If you are to create persuasive charts, you need to follow a systematic process based around the answers to certain key questions.

1. What is your key message? For example:
   - Do you want to compare different values? If so, you'll probably need to draw a bar chart of some kind.
   - Do you want to compare parts of a whole? Draw a pie chart.
   - Do you want to show trends? Draw one or more line graphs.
   - Do you want to show distributions? Use a histogram or frequency chart.

2. How much information will you show? For example:
   - Do you want to emphasise the links between two factors or are you trying to show data on many different elements?
   - Will people use the chart to get detailed information? If so you may need to show gridlines on both the vertical and horizontal axes.
   - How will you show people what the axes represent? What if the chart shows many variables? What about units?

3. Will the main points be clear to the audience? Some problems that can cause confusion are:
   - including too many elements (for example in a pie chart you may be able to class many elements as 'Other')
   - showing too many overlapping lines on a single line graph (it may be more effective to show these as a number of separate graphs)
   - using different scales or origins in related charts.

Focussing on the 'unusual'

In many work situations, the 'unusual' results are particularly important. For example, how many customers have to wait more than three minutes to be served? How many products are outside specification? How many trains arrive more than ten minutes late?

Basing your analysis on average results is a risky procedure as it risks missing the unusual. Consider a sample of 10 items of the following weights in grams: 5, 5, 5, 5, 8, 2, 5, 5, 5, 5. The average weight of 5 gm will be within a specification of between 4 and 6 gm, but that hides the fact that two items are outside that specification.

The following quotation relates to the discovery of the hole in the ozone layer over Antarctica, one of the key elements linked to global warming.

> The British Antarctic Survey had been measuring ozone in the stratosphere above Antarctica and regularly publishing the results until the early 1970s. Then, due to staff cuts, although the data was still collected, it was not analysed and published. Not until the 1980s was the data looked at again and then the alarming decrease of ozone during the Antarctic spring was discovered.
>
> To verify the information, data from a weather satellite was analysed. That too had been collecting information about ozone in the stratosphere which was not being analysed. The computer processing the information had been programmed to ignore low ozone values.

www.enfo.ie/leaflets/bs25.htm

Note the two risks that all managers face: first the risk that data will be collected but not analysed, and second that the analysis will ignore 'unusual data'. It is easy to say "That result is unusual, it must be wrong" but it is often more productive to say "That result is unusual, I wonder why?" and to investigate it further.

Activity 8
Using spreadsheets

Objective

This activity will help you to assess the use, benefits and limitations of spreadsheets to analyse and present data.

Note that the data is relatively simple and could be analysed using only a hand-held calculator. However, we suggest that you enter it into a computer spreadsheet to investigate some of the benefits and limitations of using this tool.

Task

The data in Table 3.8 shows the costs of wages, operations, and materials in four departments of the same company. It also shows the number of staff and the output for each department. Each department produces the same products, but in different geographical locations.

Department	Item	Actual rate	Rate per person	Rate per output
A	Staff	20		
A	Wages (£k)	50		
A	Operation (£k)	40		
A	Materials (£k)	60		
A	Output (k)	20		
B	Staff	35	–	1.4
B	Wages (£k)	70	2.0	2.8
B	Operation (£k)	60	1.7	2.4
B	Materials (£k)	45	1.3	1.8
B	Output (k)	25	0.7	–
C	Staff	40		
C	Wages (£k)	90		
C	Operation (£k)	60		
C	Materials (£k)	80		
C	Output (k)	45		
D	Staff	50		
D	Wages (£k)	100		
D	Operation (£k)	60		
D	Materials (£k)	90		
D	Output (k)	50		

Table 3.8 *Data on four production departments*

1. Use formulas in each of the final columns to calculate the levels of wages, operations and materials per person, and for each item of output. We've shown examples relating to Department A.

2. Add rows that show the total cost, the total cost per person, and the total cost per output.

3. Group the data so that you can most easily compare the costs of wages, of materials and so on.

4. What can you conclude from the various ways of grouping the data that you choose?

5. What would you do next?

Feedback

1. When creating the values per person, or per output, note that it makes the information clearer if you format the cells so that they contain a consistent number of decimal places (we used one decimal place). In tables as simple as this, you could easily do the calculations manually, but that will rarely be true in the real world, and anyway it will not enable you to do What-if? Calculations later.

2. As in (1), make sure that you use formulas to calculate the values, and show a suitable number of significant figures. Your table should now look like Table 3.9. This table can be used quite easily to compare total costs, but is quite difficult to interpret in relation to costs of particular items of expenditure in each department.

Department	Item	Actual rate	Rate per person	Rate per output
A	Staff	20	–	1.0
A	Wages (£k)	50	2.5	2.5
A	Operation (£k)	40	2.0	2.0
A	Materials (£k)	40	2.0	2.0
A	Output (k)	20	1.0	–
A	Total costs (£k)		6.5	6.5
B	Staff	35	–	1.4
B	Wages (£k)	70	2.0	2.8
B	Operation (£k)	60	1.7	2.4
B	Materials (£k)	45	1.3	1.8
B	Output (k)	25	0.7	–
B	Total costs (£k)		5.0	7.0
C	Staff	40	–	0.9
C	Wages (£k)	90	2.3	2.0
C	Operation (£k)	60	1.5	1.3
C	Materials (£k)	80	2.0	1.8
C	Output (k)	45	1.1	–
C	Total costs (£k)		5.8	5.1
D	Staff	50	–	1.0
D	Wages (£k)	100	2.0	2.0
D	Operation (£k)	60	1.2	1.2
D	Materials (£k)	120	2.4	2.4
D	Output (k)	50	1.0	–
D	Total costs (£k)		5.6	5.6

Table 3.9 *Data on the departments, showing costs and rate of production per person and per output*

3. Grouping the data gives Table 3.10. Note that this is sorted in two ways, first in relation to Items and then in relation to Rate per person. That makes it easy to see, for example, which department has the highest wage rates per person.

In contrast, Table 3.11 is based on the various rates per item of output.

Department	Item	Rate per person
D	Materials (£k)	2.4
A	Materials (£k)	2.0
C	Materials (£k)	2.0
B	Materials (£k)	1.3
A	Operation (£k)	2.0
B	Operation (£k)	1.7
C	Operation (£k)	1.5
D	Operation (£k)	1.2
A	Wages (£k)	2.5
C	Wages (£k)	2.3
B	Wages (£k)	2.0
D	Wages (£k)	2.0
C	Output (k)	1.1
A	Output (k)	1.0
D	Output (k)	1.0
B	Output (k)	0.7
A	Total cost (£k)	6.5
C	Total cost (£k)	5.8
D	Total cost (£k)	5.6
B	Total cost (£k)	5.0

Table 3.10 *Grouped data on the departments (based on rate per person)*

Department	Item	Rate per output
D	Materials (£k)	2.4
A	Materials (£k)	2.0
B	Materials (£k)	1.8
C	Materials (£k)	1.8
B	Operation (£k)	2.4
A	Operation (£k)	2.0
C	Operation (£k)	1.3
D	Operation (£k)	1.2
B	Wages (£k)	2.8
A	Wages (£k)	2.5
C	Wages (£k)	2.0
D	Wages (£k)	2.0
B	Total cost (£k)	7.0
A	Total cost (£k)	6.5
D	Total cost (£k)	5.6
C	Total cost (£k)	5.1

Table 3.11 *Grouped data on the departments (based on rate per output)*

4. The grouping in Table 3.10 shows a number of important facts:

   - A has the highest total cost per person, and the highest rates per person for operations and wages.

   - B and D have the lowest costs per person, they both have low wage rates, but have very different rates for materials per person.

   The grouping in Table 3.11 shows that:

   - A and B have higher total costs per item of output.

   - B has the highest wage expenditure for each item of output.

   - D has low total costs per output, even though they have the highest rates for materials.

5. It's clear from the analysis that there is a problem with Department A. It has the highest costs for each item of output, at least partly because it has high wage costs per item of output.

   It's also clear that Departments B and D are working well. What is odd is that B achieves this by having a high wage bill per output but a low wage per person (in other words they have lots of low paid staff). In contrast, D achieves its good results by spending more on its raw materials, while keeping its wages low per person and per each item of expenditure.

If you want A to improve, should you advise them to employ more low-paid staff, or to spend more on their materials? On the basis of these figures, you cannot select the best approach – it needs further investigation.

Overall, do note the key point of this activity. Simply studying the original data would not have identified either of the points about B's large staff on low wages, nor D's high expenditure on raw materials. We only discovered those two facts by analysing the data in different ways and inspecting the results. The outcomes could not have been predicted in advance.

◆ Recap

Assess the use, benefits and limitations of spreadsheets to analyse and present data.

◆ Spreadsheets have four main uses:

– tables can be used to clearly show raw data

– function tools can be used to analyse and process the data

– 'what if' calculations can be used to assess the effect of changing one or more of the variables in a situation

– chart drawing programs can be used to quickly draw a range of charts and graphs.

◆ Tables must be clearly presented and ordered, with clear headings, units and consistent, accurate insertion of data.

◆ Managers need to identify which functions, from the vast range, are relevant to their own work.

◆ Charts and graphs need to be selected carefully to analyse data and present information clearly.

◆ Throughout all analysis, the key is to look for unusual results that may highlight unsuspected problems or opportunities.

▶▶ More @

◆ Dretke, B.J. (2001) *Statistics with Microsoft® Excel* Prentice Hall is a very useful guide to using a spreadsheet to create tables and charts and the use of functions.

◆ Buglear, J. (2005) Quantitative Methods for Business: The A-Z of QM Elsevier gives useful guidance on the use of Excel, MINITAB and SPSS, linking the descriptions to specific types of analysis.

◆ There is a large range of suitable guides to project management. One suitable introductory guide is:

 – Nokes, S. (2003) *The Definitive Guide to Project Management: The Fast Track to Getting the Job Done on Time and on Budget* Prentice Hall

You will also find information on network diagrams and critical path analysis in:

 – Wilson, D. A. (2002) *Managing Information: IT for Business Process* Butterworth-Heinemann

 – Wisniewski, M. (1997) Quantitative Methods for Decision Makers Pitman

◆ The **Wikipedia** website contains a good summary of the various visual tools and links to a number of other sites, including some open-source software that you can experiment with. See:

 – http://en.wikipedia.org/wiki/Gantt_chart

 – http://en.wikipedia.org/wiki/Ishikawa_diagram

 – http://en.wikipedia.org/wiki/Flowcharts

You will find other useful guidance on various websites by searching for the relevant visual tool. One site that contains examples of many of the tools is:

 – www.skymark.com/resources/tools

4 Analytical statistics

Among the simplest examples of analytical statistics are the three types of average that you encountered earlier: mean, mode and median. These use very basic calculations to analyse data and create information that can easily be used to make decisions. Being given the weight of 500 individual products, you would find it difficult to come to any meaningful conclusions. However, knowing that the mean weight was 25 gm, you could decide how strong a box to put them in for delivery.

> **"Statistical thinking will one day be as necessary for efficient citizenship as the ability to read and write."**
> **H. G. Wells**

Unfortunately, the mean value does not tell you anything about the range of weights. Are they all in the range 20 to 30 gm, or in the range 24.5 to 25.5 gm? Does the range of weights result from variations in the quality of the materials? Are there any gradual trends in the quality of the output? To answer questions like these you need to use rather more sophisticated statistics, as described in this theme.

If you haven't used some of these techniques before, you may find them rather confusing. The key is to remember that our aim is to look at how each one could be used, so that you can decide what advantages they could each give you in your work. Rather like working on a new computer package for the first time, once you start to use a new statistical technique in practice it quickly becomes simple and automatic.

When you have identified which techniques are most helpful in your own work, you will then need to find out more in the statistics textbooks or by using your spreadsheet formulas. Further references are provided in the More@ section at the end of the theme.

In this theme you will assess the use, benefits and limitations of:

1. the statistical techniques of index numbers, time series analysis, and correlation and regression analysis

2. techniques linked to probability and sampling, including distribution theory and standard deviation, estimation, significance testing and statistical process control

3. operations research techniques, including linear programming, queuing theory and simulation.

Statistical tools

We start by looking at a number of statistical tools that can be used to study the relationship between two variables for example, the analysis of consumer expenditure in relation to income, or the relationship between doses of a drug and survival rates. Often one of the two variables used within the analysis is time. Data collected over time is very important for the successful performance of organisations. It enables them to monitor changes in the business environment such as levels of consumer spending or the progress that they are making; sales, profits etc.

Two analyses that use time as one of the variables are index numbers and time series analyses.

Index numbers

"The FTSE 100 Index went up by 3 points today." "The cost of living index has risen by two per cent." Similar comments appear on the news every day, but what exactly does the word 'index' mean?

Index numbers measure the value of an item (or group of items) at a particular point in time as a percentage of an item (or group of items) at another point in time. They are commonly used in business and economics as indicators of changing business or economic activity.

Let's assume that a product was worth £1000 at the end of 2000 and that its price has risen by £50 every year since then. At the end of 2001 the new price will be £1050 and the index price rise based on the 2000 base year will be:

$$\frac{1050}{1000} = 1.050$$

By the end of 2002, the index price rise, again based on 2000 will be:

$$\frac{1100}{1000} = 1.100$$

If, on the other hand, we decided to call 2001 the base year the price index in 2002 will be:

$$\frac{1100}{1050} = 1.048$$

Index numbers can thus be used to compare changes in different items, provided all the calculations use the same base year.

Index numbers are particularly useful where we want to assess the average change for a number of items. One example is the cost of living index, based on the cost of a basket of goods that the average household is thought to need each week. Table 4.1 shows the costs of three items, the number that are purchased, and the total costs.

Table 4.1 *A model of the cost of living index*

Based on the figures in Table 4.1, the cost of living index =

$$\frac{835}{790} = 1.057$$

The cost of living has increased by 5.7 per cent.

Item	Cost in 2000 (p)	Cost in 2001 (p)	Number bought	Total cost 2000 (p)	Total cost 2001 (p)
Apples	150	155	2	300	310
Bananas	130	135	3	390	405
Carrots	50	60	2	100	120
			Overall total	790	835

One common use of index number is to remove the effect of inflation on prices or costs. For example a company that sells its products for £100 in 2000 could think it was doing very well to sell exactly the same product for £110 in 2005. But if all prices had been inflated by 2% each year, the company would actually be selling the product more cheaply in real terms.

The price of £100 would need to increase to

$100 \times 1.02 \times 1.02 \times 1.02 \times 1.02 \times 1.02 = 110.41$

to cover the increased costs linked to inflation.

Indexing gives managers a chance to compare changes in very different variables. For example, hospital managers may want to investigate trends in overall patient numbers, the doctor/patient ratio, and the contact time spent per patient. Line graphs of the three sets of data would be useful, but indexing could give ever more useful information. By indexing each variable, say to levels in 2000, management could easily reach conclusions about relative movement, such as "The doctor patient ratio has increased by 20% but contact time has only increased by 5%".

Indexing gives people a useful guide to changes in the value of items, or groups of items. On the other hand, indexes can be relatively easily manipulated. For example, you could create high levels of the index by basing them on a base from a period of particularly low values. Opponents accused Chancellor Gordon Brown of manipulating the figures when he changed the base year used for calculating the cost of living index.

Time series analysis

The easiest way to assess how a variable varies with time is to draw a line graph. Unfortunately, very few variables actually vary consistently and give clear graphs. Think of sales of ice cream. There will typically be:

♦ a trend, perhaps a long term increase in sales over a number of years

♦ seasonal elements (involving periods of days or weeks), for example with people buying more ice cream during the summer, or at the weekend

♦ cyclical elements, perhaps with people changing their tastes over a three or four year cycle

♦ random or residual elements, caused by unexpected warm periods in the autumn, or year-round sales to people with particular dietary needs.

Time series analysis aims to identify specific components of overall performance, for example removing the last three effects and looking for long term trends, or focusing only on seasonal elements.

Table 4.2 shows customer numbers in a large store each day over a four-week period.

Shown in Figure 4.1, there is clearly a 'seasonal' element with a gradual increase each week from Monday to Sunday. But there is also a gradual upward trend – sales each week are all slightly higher than they were in the previous week.

One way to analyse the gradual upward trend is to find the **moving average** of weekly customer numbers. Calculating the mean number of customers in each week gives 8.0, 8.7, 10.0 and 11.1, confirming that there is a gradual upwards trend. You could also use the *Trend* tool in your spreadsheet to analyse the original data – the results of that analysis are shown by the gradually-rising, straight line in Figure 4.1.

Notice that the period of the seasonal element here was 7 days. This could be easily predicted for a retail outlet, but you may have to search rather more carefully in other situations.

Day	M	T	W	T	F	S	S	M	T	W	T	F	S	S	M	T	W	T	F
Customers (000's)	4	5	6	8	10	11	12	5	6	7	7	11	12	13	6	7	8	10	12

Table 4.2 *Customer numbers each day over 4 weeks*

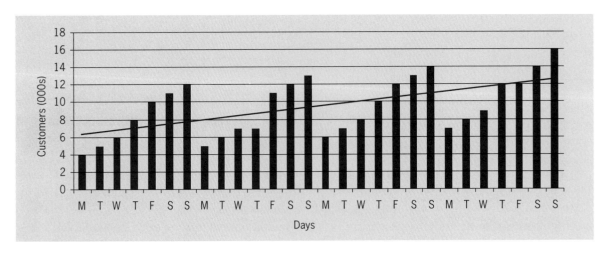

Figure 4.1 *Customer numbers each day over 4 weeks*

Correlation and regression analysis

In the example of the customer numbers in the retail store, there seems to be a link between customer numbers and the days of week. We now need to look a little more closely at the words "seems to be a link between".

The simplest way of finding links is to use scatter diagrams. Consider the following scenario.

A company is trying to decide how many ice cream vans to put on the road. It has records of the number of vans used on particular days and the revenue, shown in Table 4.3.

Number of vans	Revenue (£K)
2	2
3	1
3	3
3	4
4	2
4	4
5	3
5	5
6	2
7	5
7	6
7	7
8	2
8	4
9	7

Table 4.3 *Revenue from ice cream vans*

Inspecting the data shows little, but the situation becomes clearer if the data is shown on a scatter chart (see Figure 4.2). This does confirm that increasing the number of vans tends to increase the revenue. But do note that the rule is not perfect – there is a lot of variation in the results. For example one result shows 3 vans making more money than 5, 7 or 8 vans.

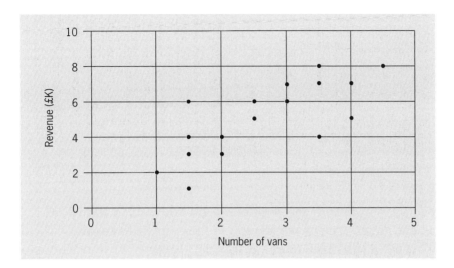

Figure 4.2 *A scatter diagram*

A number of terms related to scatter diagrams are given specific meanings. In this example:

◆ the number of vans is known as the **independent variable**

◆ the revenue, which depends at least partly on the number of vans, is known as the **dependent variable**

◆ there is said to be a **positive correlation** between the number of vans and the revenue – the results slope gradually upwards.

Other types of correlation also occur, for example:

◆ negative correlation is shown by a downwards sloping chart
 – this could apply to the relationship between production levels and numbers of employees on sick leave

◆ zero correlation occurs when there is no connection between the two variables, for example between people's attendance record and the initial letter of their surname – there would seem to be no general trend in the scatter chart.

Having drawn a scatter diagram, it is often helpful to draw a **regression line**, which represents the points on the scatter diagram. Figure 4.3 shows a typical example for a negative correlation.

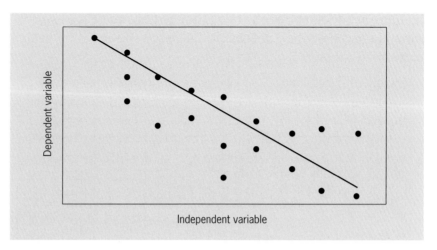

Figure 4.3 *A regression line showing a negative correlation*

Finding the gradient and position of this line requires statistical analysis tools . The most common of these, the **least squares method**, is described in the various statistics texts listed in the *More @* section. Using a spreadsheet you can also use tools that may be called TREND or SLOPE.

Unfortunately, the regression line itself does not show how well the data fits the line. Compare the two sets of data shown in Figure 4.4. The widely spread data in Figure 4.4.A would be represented by exactly the same regression line as the closely correlated data in Figure 4.4(B).

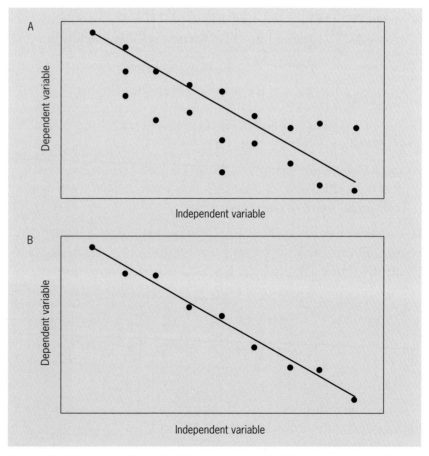

Figure 4.4 *Two contrasting sets of data represented by the same regression line*

A number of methods can be used to assess how closely the results correspond to the regression line. For example:

1. **Pearson product moment correlation** considers each of the independent variables, and compares the actual value of the dependent variable with the value predicted by the regression line. A value of + 1 shows that the y-data is perfectly correlated with the x-data. A value of zero shows no relationship between the data and a value of -1 shows a perfect negative correlation. Try using the PEARSON function on your spreadsheet with the values in Table 4.3, then investigate the effect of changing some of the values.

2. **Spearman rank correlation** is used where the actual values are not known, but you do know the variables in rank order (for example Shell is the largest, followed by Esso, BP etc). The aim of measuring rank correlation is to investigate whether there is a correlation between the two sets of rank orders. Does the fact that Manager A is good at financial management predict anything (positive or negative) about his or her people skills?

Activity 9
Selecting suitable statistical tools to analyse data

Objective

This activity will help you to assess the use, benefits and limitations of the statistical techniques of index numbers, time series analysis, and correlation and regression analysis.

Task

A company records its sales per quarter, as shown in the first three rows of Table 4.4.

1. Using a spreadsheet to create a chart of the results, what can you conclude about overall levels of sales?

2. What does a trend line on the chart show?

3. What does a moving average of sales show about trends in sales?

4. If the mean sales for year 1 are taken as the base, what is the sales index for years 2 and 3?

5. One manager has a theory that the variable nature of sales is linked to levels of holiday bookings made during each quarter. These are shown in row 4 of Table 4.4. Do you agree with the manager?

Year		1				2				3		
Quarter	1st	2nd	3rd	4th	1st	2nd	3rd	4th	1st	2nd	3rd	4th
Sales (£100k)	4	8	6	5	5	9	7	6	7	11	9	8
Holiday bookings	60	80	80	90	70	90	120	90	80	90	100	90

Table 4.4 *Quarterly sales figures*

6. Finally, having seen how these techniques could be used in our imaginary company, spend some time thinking how they could be used in your own work. Look in particular for ways in which you could use the techniques to identify unexpected results and links.

Feedback

1. The chart is shown in Figure 4.5, showing annual variation but an overall rise in sales.

2. The trend line also suggests that there is a gradual increase in sales.

3. Table 4.5 shows the moving average for sales per quarter. Again, this shows a gradual rise in sales.

4. Calculating the two values of the sales index, based on year 1, gives:

$$\frac{6.75}{5.57} = 1.17 \text{ for year 2, and}$$

$$\frac{8.75}{5.75} = 1.52 \text{ for year 3.}$$

Note that these also become progressively larger.

5. The scatter chart in Figure 4.6 suggests that an increase in holiday bookings occurs at the same time as an increase in sales of the company's product. But note that it is not clear which factor affects the other, or whether it is coincidence.

If the product is travel magazines, then the increase in holiday bookings may result to some extent from an increase in sales of magazines. On the other hand, if the company's product is suntan cream, the causation could be in the other direction. Or there may be no direct link. If the product is overcoats, a increase in sales of overcoats and holidays may both result from periods of cold weather.

6. This section of the activity is the most important, but the one in which we can give least feedback. Every one of these tools is useful, but gives specific information. On the one hand, it is important to identify which tools you will use

repeatedly to carry out standard tasks. On the other hand, using different tools will often provide the 'unexpected information' that highlights problems or opportunities.

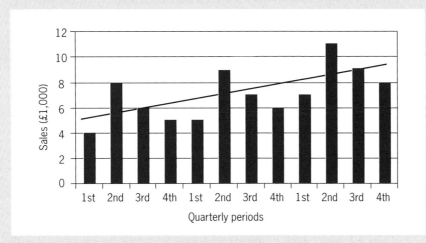

Figure 4.5 *Chart showing sales per quarter and trend line*

Year		1				2				3		
Quarter	1st	2nd	3rd	4th	1st	2nd	3rd	4th	1st	2nd	3rd	4th
Sales	4	8	6	5	5	9	7	6	7	11	9	8
Moving average per quarter			5.75				6.75				8.75	

Table 4.5 *Quarterly sales figures and moving average*

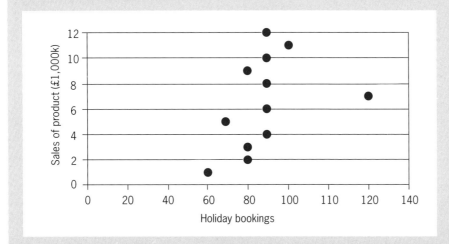

Figure 4.6 *Scatter chart*

Probability and sampling

The first section of this theme looked at ways of analysing the relationship between two different attributes such as changes in sales over time. We looked at how you can assess whether there is a correlation between the attributes, for example, if sales of a car rise, is that because of a good advertising campaign, because prices have been reduced, or for some totally different reason?

Next we look at probability theory; the aspect of statistics that is about finding out how likely something is to happen. We start with simple probability. If an assembly line operator makes an error on one car in ten, and a quality inspector misses one in ten errors, how likely is it that a faulty car will be passed? We then see how samples can be used to give information about the whole population. And finally we describe the use of probability theory in statistical process control, for example showing how samples taken from output can be used to assess overall performance.

Probability

If you toss a coin, there is a probability of one in two, 0.5 or 50% that it will come down tails. For a six-sided dice, the probability of throwing a 2 is one in six, in other words:

$$\frac{1}{6} = 0.167, \textit{ or } 16.7\%$$

Managers rarely toss coins to make decisions, but they do need to understand how probabilities affect their work. A manager may know that one supplier delivers in the morning 3 times out of every 4 (or probability 75%), and that team member Jim works on 3 days out of 5 (or 60%).

What is the probability that the supplier will deliver in the morning on a day when Jim is at work? It looks quite likely, since both the separate probabilities are over 50%.

But is it that simple? The problem is known as compound probability – both conditions must apply at the same time. The overall probability is given by multiplying each probability together. There is only a 1 in 12 chance of tossing a tails (1 in 2) and throwing a 2 (1 in 6) at the same time. For the manager's problem, the probability of both events being true is:

$$\frac{3}{4} \times \frac{3}{5} = 0.45, \textit{ or } 45\%$$

In other words, although each individual probability is over 50%, the chance of getting both of them is only 45%. This example highlights the need to make decisions based on careful analysis of accurate information whenever possible, rather than making decisions based on, say "a fifty-fifty chance". The probability of success based on two 'fifty-fifty' probabilities is one in four.

Decision trees

Many management decisions depend on careful analysis of the likely benefits of a number of alternative strategies. For example Figure 4.7 shows a decision tree analysing three options for an existing company: to invest in expansion, to create a franchise, and to sell the business. Managers have estimated the probability of the market increasing, staying level and decreasing, and calculated the pay off for each of the various options.

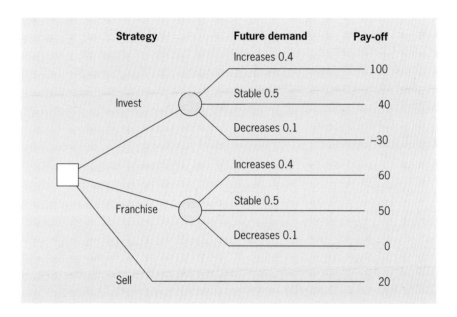

Figure 4.7 *A decision tree*   Source: Buglear (Elsevier)

Based on this decision tree the expected monetary value of investing is:

$(0.4 \times 100) + (0.5 \times 40) + 0.1 \times (-30)) = £57m.$

Similar calculations show the expected monetary value of franchising is £49m and for selling is £20m. Overall, the techniques therefore suggest that investing will be the best approach. As always, the managers then need to consider the mathematical outcomes in common sense terms. Investing will lose money if demand decreases, but there will be no losses if they franchise or sell. The management need to check that their figure of 0.1 probability of a decreasing market is realistic.

Calculating probabilities

In that example, managers had to make an estimate of a probability. In many cases, however, it is possible to calculate probabilities. For example Figure 4.8 shows the probability that a coin will fall heads a stated number of times out of 12 throws. For example it shows that the probability of getting heads 6 times out of twelve is 0.25.

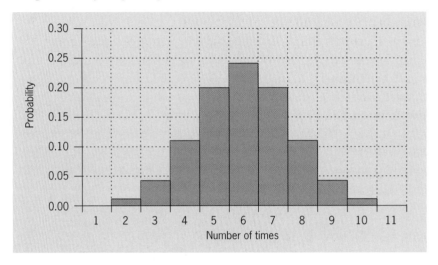

Figure 4.8 *Probability of getting heads after 12 throws*

As you increase the number of throws the shape becomes progressively closer to a bell-shaped curve. This is known as a **normal distribution.** A normal distribution is a term which is used to describe a set of data where most of the examples are clustered around the average while relatively fewer examples tend to one extreme or the other.

If you looked at normally distributed data on a graph, it would look something like Figure 4.9. The x-axis is the variable in question; product weight, pounds earned, calories consumed etc.. And the y-axis is the number of datapoints for each value on the x-axis. In other words, the number of bags of sugar that weigh x grams, the number of households that earn x pounds or the number of people who eat x calories.

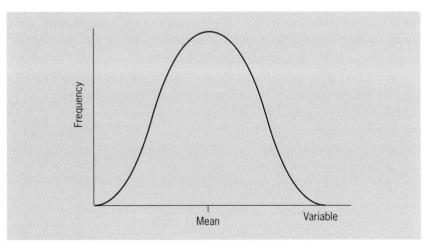

Figure 4.9 *A normal distribution*

Two key statistics can help a manager to analyse a set of data: the average value and the range or spread of the values. Where the distribution is normal, these are represented by the mean and the **standard deviation** (σ), which can be calculated using standard formulae available in spreadsheets.

The standard deviation is a statistic that tells you how tightly all the various values are clustered around the mean. When the values are spread apart, the standard deviation is relatively large and the bell curve is relatively flat. When the values are pretty tightly bunched together, the standard deviation is much smaller and the bell shaped curve is steep.

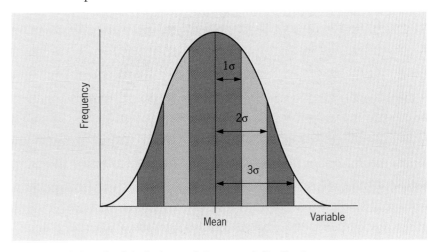

Figure 4.10 *Standard deviation and the normal distribution curve*

Statisticians have calculated that:

◆ One standard deviation from the mean in either direction (shown on the graph) accounts for around 68% of the total population.

◆ Two standard deviations away from the mean account for around 95% of the population.

◆ Three standard deviations account for around 99 percent of the population.

The standard deviation enables you to make a prediction about the likely range of values that may occur. For example a bag of sugar may be marked with a mean weight 1000 g. If the producer knows from experience that the standard deviation is 5 g, then it is reasonable to predict that:

◆ 68% of bags lie in the range 995 to 1005 g (in other words 1000 ± 5 g)

◆ 95% of bags are in the range 990 to 1010 g (within two standard deviations of the mean)

◆ less than 1% of bags weigh less than 985 g or more than 1015 g (more than three standard deviations of the mean).

Sampling

Having seen that the mean and the standard deviation give useful information, the next question is to ask how they can be measured. It is, of course, possible to measure every item individually but that can be a very expensive option. Consider two extreme examples. A surgeon installing a plastic replacement heart valve must know that every one has been individually tested. But a builder's merchants could not justify the cost of carrying out individual checks on every plastic tap washer.

In practice, it is usual to take a sample and assume that the results mirror the properties of the whole population. Managers need to balance two factors in deciding what sample size to take:

◆ the need to take a sample that accurately reflects the population

◆ the need to keep sampling costs (in time and resources) to a minimum.

A manager may want to find out how many miles, on average, staff travel to work. It might be possible to sample the whole population, perhaps finding out that the mean is 10 miles. In a large organisation this would be a costly exercise and a more cost-effective option is to sample.

If the manager asked just two people and got the answers of 9 and 13, the mean value would be inaccurate at 11. To decrease the chance that the sample will be off the mark, the manager needs to add more people to the sample.

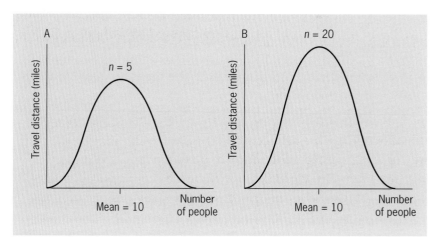

Figure 4.11 *Sampling, using different sample sizes*

If the manager had asked 5 people and then calculated the mean, it is more likely that the answer would be closer to the actual average of 10. Note how the frequency curve becomes narrower.

The effect is likely to become more marked if samples of 20 people are used.

It's common sense that using a larger sample will enable you to make the most accurate predictions about the target population. But how large does the sample size need to be?

The standard error is a calculation that enables us to anticipate the margin of error associated with a sample. The formula that describes the relationship is:

The margin of error in a sample = 1 / square root of the number of people in the sample.

The formula is derived from the standard deviation of the proportion of times that a researcher gets a sample "right".

The range of uses of sampling is enormous. It's standard practice in many situations, for example in production lines to check quality, in roadside surveys of commercial vehicles, in surveying public attitudes for marketing, and so on. As a manager using the technique, or using the results obtained by others, the key is to consider the likely error of the results. For example surveys of people's voting intentions may be presented as "Party A leads party B by 2 percentage points", but that information is fairly meaningless if both sets of figures have a standard error of 3%.

Confidence in your results

Once you know the results for your sample, your next job is to use them to predict the values for the population as a whole. The key question to ask is how confident are you that the values you have calculated for your sample mirror the values for the population as a whole? For example a survey of 500 consumers in a postcode area might show that 260 of them use a particular detergent. The market share based on the sample is:

> "An approximate answer to the right question is worth a good deal more than the exact answer to an approximate problem."
> John Tukey (1962)

$$\frac{260}{500} = 0.52 = 52\%$$

But is it reasonable to assume that 52% of the total population in the postcode use the detergent? Statisticians maintain that the best way of using sample information to predict population measures is to use **interval estimation**, also known as **confidence limits.** Interval estimations are usually calculated so that we can be 95% confident that the population measure lies between the two values.

Using our detergent example, given the number in the sample, the 95% interval estimate can then be calculated to be 0.0437. In other words you can be 95% certain that the actual market share is in the range 0.2 ± 0.0437, or using percentages 52% ± 4.37%.

Increasing the level of confidence requires the use of larger samples, but this increases the costs and time involved. To give 99% certainty within ± ½ % needs a sample size of 12,608.

Sampling and using sample results to estimate the characteristics of a population involves a good understanding of statistics. As you have seen already, you may come across many terms that are used in very specific ways, such as standard deviation, standard error and interval estimate. All three of these terms relate to the range of a set values, but actually give rather different information. If you do not have a statistical background, a safe option is only to compare like with like – if you are considering two sets of data, if possible focus on the standard deviation of both.

These techniques are certainly too useful to leave only to the statisticians. It is easy to calculate means, but it gives very little useful information if you do not know the range of values that they actually represent.

Significance testing

Having taken a sample, and used it to draw a conclusion, how can you then decide whether that conclusion is significant? Think of the example of a production manager who wants to discover whether a production line is producing too many defective items.

The expected number of defectives is 5% of total production. The situation is assessed by monitoring performance, taking samples of 1000 items. If there are more than 50 defective items in first sample, what does this mean?

Since the occurrence of defectives is random, it certainly does not mean that the manager should immediately stop the production line. The manager must consider two possibilities – the failure rate is at the 5% expected level, or the actual failure rate is greater than 5%.

The manager can then analyse four possible scenarios:

1. think the failure rate is correct when it actually is correct

2. think the failure rate is incorrect when it actually is incorrect

3. think the failure rate is correct when it is actually higher

4. think the failure rate is higher when it is actually acceptable.

(1) and (2) do not pose any problem. The manager would have taken a suitable action in both cases. The difficulties come with situations (3) and (4). If the manager assumes the rate is correct, the company will continue to output products outside specification. If the manager stops the production line when there is actually no problem, there will be additional costs for no good reason.

The manager's decision will generally depend on the product being considered. Is quality a key factor (for example it would be in the manufacture of medical supplies or food products)? If so then the manager should stop production. In the case of nuts and bolts, quality may be less of a consideration so the manager should probably continue production.

The occurrence of defectives will follow a normal distribution. Knowing this, the manager can use statistical techniques to calculate suitable limits on production. For example the manager may decide to stop the production process when the number of defective items reaches 65 per thousand. The process of significance testing involves a number of statistical calculations, and is generally left to statisticians. However, managers do need to be aware of the main points, as outlined above.

We've used an example based on a production process, but the same approach could be used to assess the significance of any sample. If 20 people from a sample of 100 potential customers say that a product is overpriced, is this significant? What if 200 people from a sample of 300 potential customers say the same thing? The larger the sample, the more significant the findings.

Statistical process control

The earlier discussion of distributions, samples and significance all related to static situations. A manager had collected data about products or other outputs, analysed the data, and then reached a conclusion about what action to take next.

In many work situations, particularly in production industries, there is a constant flow of output. Decisions about solving problems or maintaining quality must be taken on a continuous basis. To do this needs a development of the earlier statistical methods.

Samples may be taken at key stages during the process and subjected to a series of quality inspections. The results of these inspections are shown on control charts, giving the manager a chance to assess how quality varies throughout the process. This enables the manager to identify:

◆ changes in quality over time

◆ stages of the process at which significant deterioration in quality occurs

◆ whether changes in quality occur by chance or as a result of external causes such as changes in the performance of equipment.

In all operations there will inevitably be some variation in products or outputs. The causes fall into two categories:

◆ **Chance** or **usual** variation generally occurs at random and comparatively little can be done about it. Examples of the causes might include random variations in the feedstocks used, or fluctuations in the power supply.

◆ **Assignable** or **unusual** variation occurs less frequently and usually represents a measurable change or trend. As its name suggests, assignable variation can normally be traced to some external cause. Typical causes might include wear in a machine, changes in personnel, the use of a new feedstock, unusually high operating temperatures and so on.

Quality controllers define **control limits** at each stage of the process, based on the theory of probability distributions covered above. If variations are random:

♦ the product variable should lie within three standard deviations on either side of the mean; any variation which occurs beyond these limits has probably occurred from some assignable cause so action must be taken

♦ 95.4% of the time the product variable will be within two standard deviations of the mean; many managers will set a warning limit at this level.

Think of a company producing plastic tubes designed to have length 500 mm with standard deviation 4 mm. The quality controller could decide that action would be needed if actual output was outside 3 standard deviations of the mean. In other words, production would continue only if the samples were within the range 488 to 512 mm.

At one-hour intervals, tests are made on the length of a sample tube and the results are plotted on the chart, as shown in Figure 4.12.

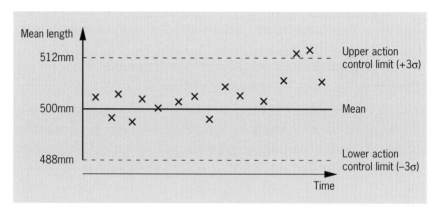

Figure 4.12 *A control chart*

This control chart shows that the samples at the beginning of the process are all within the control limits. After a time, however, there is a gradual rise in the mean values and some of the products lie outside the acceptable range. The gradual rise in values suggests that there is an assignable variation which must be investigated.

Statistical process control is often used at a number of times during a process, for example taking samples from:

♦ inputs to the process before they are accepted

♦ part-manufactured products at key stages of the production process

♦ outputs before delivery to the customer.

When planning a system of control charts, or any other quality control mechanism, the manager must clearly identify the key factors which affect quality. The key quality factors can be classified as:

- **variables**, such as length, weight, diameter or volume
- **attributes**, for example the number of rivets or the number of bottles with correct labels.

Control charts for variables are based on mean values and variation about the mean. In the previous example, plastic tubes were acceptable if they were within three standard deviations of a mean of 500mm. Other examples might include the volume of beer in a can, the elasticity of a drive belt, or the weight of toner in a photocopier cartridge.

As we did in the discussion of statistical significance, we've used an example based on a production process. But we could just as easily have based it on many other types of measurable output. Examples might include the time that call centre staff take to respond to a call, the accuracy of data entry operators or copy editors checking spelling, or the number complaints made about hotel staff.

Control charts for attributes must be based on the size of the total sample and the number of defective items within that sample. One quality control used on encyclopaedias involves checking for spelling mistakes; an acceptable quality might be for fewer than five spelling mistakes per ten page sample. A telephone operator might be assessed over an hour period by counting how many times the phone was unanswered after five rings. In both cases there is a clear upper control limit: over five incorrect words, or over five calls, would be unacceptable. Control charts for attributes may show the percentage or actual number of defective items in a sample.

As with all of the earlier examples of statistical techniques, it is important to understand the general principles of how statistical process control works. The details of the statistics, for example of calculating a suitable range for the control limits, are more complex than we can cover here, though they are described in the textbooks listed in the *More @* section.

Activity 10
Assessing probability and sampling techniques

Objective

This activity will help you to assess the use, benefits and limitations of the techniques linked to probability and sampling, including distribution theory and standard deviation, estimation, significance testing and statistical process control.

Task

Worldwide International produce electronic equipment in five locations around the world. Managers at each location have been told that they are to develop their own management approaches but must aim to minimise overall costs. Performance at each location will be assessed against 10 criteria each year.

1. Which of the techniques described in this theme would be particularly useful when initially comparing the 5 locations? What factors would you need to consider when using the techniques?

2. After three years, one manager says that her location's success is based on the fact that they only employ full-time staff. Other locations have varying mixes of part-time and full-time employees. How could you assess whether the manager's comments were valid?

3. When the topic of part-time working is discussed, other managers talk about some related problems that would occur if they reduced the number of part-time workers. You decide to use a decision tree to structure the discussion. What factors would you initially expect to see on the tree?

4. "Now that we do produce high quality goods, we could reduce costs by reducing the amount of sampling that we do." In a company producing standard products over long periods, this seems a sensible approach. Is it?

As with all the techniques that we describe, the key aim is for you to assess what value they may have in your own work, and to assess the advantages and disadvantages of each. Having considered some of them in relation to the Worldwide scenario, now spend a few minutes assessing the possible benefits and relevance of each of the techniques in this theme.

Feedback

1. Central managers have a complex task if they are going to compare the 5 locations against 10 criteria, and presumably make allowance for changes in factors such as costs of resources, inflation and exchange rates. They will almost certainly need to use some form of indexing. This will allow them to assess, for example, how costs of materials or wages have increased each year, without needing to calculate the absolute values of those costs. It will also allow them to easily calculate changes in factors that link to many elements, for example changes in overall costs will depend on changes in materials, wages, exchange rates, taxation, and so on.

An alternative approach would be to use graphical methods, for example representing costs on a line graph. Here there is a risk that underlying trends will be hidden by seasonal factors. While managers in Europe or the USA can expect an increase in sales around Christmas time, seasonal variation are likely to be very different in, say, a Muslim or Buddhist country. It would also be necessary to assess random effects such as inflation or changes in the exchange rate.

2. You would be looking for a correlation between 'success' and the proportion of full-time staff. Without any further information, let us assume that the manager means achieving the aim of minimising costs.

    The most suitable technique would be significance testing. Is the reduction in costs a result of the number of full-time staff or are there other linked factors. For example are both factors actually results of better working conditions, or factors related to the national or organisational culture at each location?

3. The three options are "Increase full-time numbers", "Reduce full-time numbers", and "Make no change". In each case you could assess the likely effect on costs. For example on some of the locations, there is a major risk that not allowing part-time working will incur fines and affect the company's public image. What is the probability of these effects, and how can you calculate their financial costs?

4. As a Worldwide manager, you need to be careful with this comment. Firstly, because sampling is the only way of ensuring that the quality of production remains high. If you reduce the number of samples, there is a risk of creating poor quality output. The costs of recalling poor quality goods is far higher than the cost of sampling.

    Secondly for statistical reasons. The theory of sampling assumes that the sample will reflect the whole population. But the sample must always be stated with a standard error, and reducing the size of the samples will increase the standard error. Based on a sample of 90 items you could perhaps say that 95% of the sample lie in the range 200 ± 8 kg. If the sample size is reduced to 10 items, you could only say that 95% lie in the range 200 ± 24 kg. It may be that that range is acceptable, but you cannot decide to reduce the sampling size without considering the effect on the standard error.

Operations research techniques

Operations research techniques are used to ensure that large organisations make effective use of money, materials, equipment, and people. You've already seen one example, where decision trees can be used to make decisions in complex situations, and the boundary between operations research techniques and the previous topic of statistical analysis is often rather blurred.

In this section we will describe three techniques:

◆ queuing theory, which aims to predict the average waiting time and average length of time people or materials are in a queue

◆ simulation, modelling a business operation

◆ linear programming, focusing on the problem of selecting the best solution within a number of limiting constraints.

Queuing theory

Queuing theory looks at the range of variables that can affect a queue, and predicts the likely outcomes, primarily the number of elements in the queue and the time that one item takes to work through the queue. Note that we will use the term 'element' since a queue may be made up of people, materials waiting for processing, products waiting to be delivered, payments to be made, and so on. You may also come across the important topic of queuing in relation to data being transferred in a computer network. Many of the complaints about slow computers or telephone lines actually relate to queues of data waiting to pass through a key junction.

The key factors to consider in a queuing system are:

◆ the distribution of arrival times

◆ the distribution of times needed to service each element

◆ the number of servicing units

◆ the configuration of the service units (for example whether one element can be serviced by one unit, or must visit many units).

As an example, when queuing at your local post office, you will probably take a shorter time overall if you arrive at a quiet time, if most people only want to buy one postage stamp, if there are lots of people working at the counter, and if you can collect your postage stamp and pay for it at the same counter.

However, many queuing experience are not so simple, so a number of different approaches may be tried. For example, should everyone start off in the same queue, or should a separate queue form in front of each counter? Would it be more efficient to have separate queues for small purchases only? Would it help for everyone to be given an invoice and then go to a single pay point?

To assess the likely effect of each approach, managers need first to make a number of estimates and predictions. For example, by sampling current arrival times it is possible to assess the probability that any one item will arrive at a particular time. You can also estimate how long it will take to carry out different transactions and the probability of each transaction, and of various combinations of transactions.

Based on those estimates and predictions, it is possible to create a model of the possible outcomes for each of the various number and configurations of the service units. As you can imagine, this will often be a highly repetitive and lengthy task, so in practice it is carried out using a computer program.

Do note that the output will itself only give output in terms of probabilities. For example, past data can be used to predict hospital emergency referrals, but cannot allow for unusual situations like a major accident. Output from a production unit can be predicted on the basis on individual worker output, numbers of workers, input of materials and so on, but cannot predict a major closedown during a lengthy power cut.

As you have seen, queuing models are generally used to assess possible throughput rates, but they are also useful at identifying possible bottlenecks (or choke-points). A bottleneck is a crucial point in the process which limits performance, such as the narrow exit from a sports stadium that limits how fast people can leave in an emergency, or the slow-working specialist who must check every worker's output.

Queuing models can also be used to plan ways of using facilities more effectively. Think of a hospital car park. Many staff will arrive between 8:00 and 9:00, those who are attending as outpatients will generally be expected to arrive before 10:00, and some people visiting in-patients may want to visit before going to work. By predicting the numbers of cars arriving during each quarter hour period, managers would probably find that car park entry was most effective if outpatients were asked not to arrive before 9:00, and visitors were asked not to arrive before 10:00. The managers could then decide on an arrivals policy based on car park efficiency and all of the other relevant factors.

An alternative to modelling is to experiment. For example, a supermarket manager might be unsure how many checkout staff are needed at different times on each day of the week. One approach would involve varying the numbers of staff and observing the length of queues. A second approach would be to have a minimum number of staff operating checkouts, but to hold spare staff in reserve. Unfortunately, both these approaches have major disadvantages. The first risks annoying customers, the second means paying people to do nothing. Given a few preliminary sampling exercises, it should not be too difficult to use modelling and so avoid both problems.

Simulation

Queuing theory is one example of a simulation. Where most analytical techniques aim to find a solution, simulations can only provide further information. In the Post Office example, they can give information about the likely lengths of queues for different counter numbers and configurations. In the hospital parking example, they can predict the lengths of queues at different times of the morning.

More generally, simulations are used to assess the effects of many variables, where the effects of the variables can only be predicted. Consider, for example, a travel firm. They may have data showing past performance, for example showing numbers, destinations, income, costs, and so on. They can also make estimates of future trends, for example an increase in numbers of people taking holidays in a particular country, changes in group size, typical weather in different seasons, increases in air fares, changes in exchange rates, etc.

Simulation techniques could then be used to predict the outcomes under many different conditions. For example, predicting profit levels if the exchange rate fell by 10% while average incomes of one segment of the market increased by 8% and air fares rose by 5%. Having made that calculation, managers could then assess the effect if there was a 40% drop in travel following a terrorist attack.

If simulation techniques are to be effective, they must be based on large amounts of data. Typical calculations involve generating random numbers that fit the probabilities of the various variables. As a result, the techniques are only practicable if carried out using a computer. To test the validity of the model, it is usual to run historic data and assess whether the model accurately predicts changes that actually occurred.

One of the earliest uses of these techniques occurred in the 1930s when researchers assessed the effect of many variables on the manufacture of cotton. How would the incidence of faults in cloth be affected by, for example, changing humidity or changes in tension of the yarn during production?

More recent examples of situations where modelling is particularly useful include:

♦ predicting the number of insurance claims that householders or motorists are likely to make in a given period

♦ comparing different ways of increasing lager production in the 1980s, by considering changes in tank size, temperatures, alternative pipe routing, and so on.

Linear programming

Linear programming looks at the question of constraints. What is it that is actually limiting effectiveness or output? Do we need more staff, a larger workplace, or better materials?

Imagine a situation in which your company produces two liquids, HighConc and LowConc. It wants to maximise its output of LowConc but within the four following key constraints:

a) The total output per day must not exceed 5000 litres.

b) The maximum output of LowConc is 3000 litres.

c) The maximum output of HighConc is 4000 litres.

d) The output of HighConc must be at least twice the output of LowConc.

The difficulty here is the large number of relevant factors, all of which must be satisfied. You could, of course, try experimenting with particular values and see if you can find a pair that work. For example, what if you produced 2100 litres of HighConc and 1000 litres of LowConc? It's not difficult to show that this agrees with all the constraints, but it's almost certainly not the maximum output.

To find the maximum value, we've shown the constraints on a chart (see Figure 4.13). Note that each of the lines is labelled to show the relevant constraint, for example line (a) shows that total output must never exceed 5000 litres. The area that is acceptable is shaded.

The chart shows that you could produce a maximum volume of 1667 litres of LowConc and 3333 litres of HighConc. Any other value will either produce less LowConc or break one or more of the constraints.

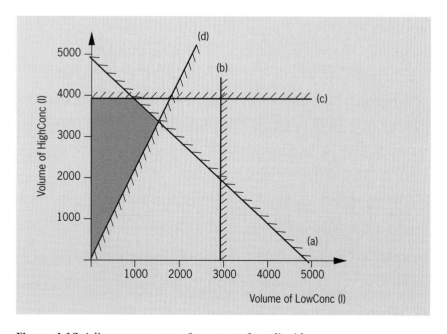

Figure 4.13 *A linear programme for output of two liquids*

Of course, few practical example can be solved in such a simple way. For example we did not consider the question of cost in the two liquids' example.

On the other hand, you may also have realised that, once you have drawn the chart, this problem can be solved mathematically. Using the symbol H for the volume of HighConc and L for volume of LowConc, the maximum output of LowConc occurs when the line:

H = 2L (constraint d)

crosses the line

H + L = 5000 (constraint a).

Remembering some school mathematics, these two equations can be solved to give:

H = 3333 and L = 1667.

Other uses of linear programming

As well as identifying the optimum solution, linear programming can be used to identify the key factors that affect performance. Looking again at Figure 4.12 it's clear that constraint (b) has no effect on the outcome. There is no benefit in having resources ready for a possible output of 3000 litres of LowConc. Given the other three constraints, the output of LowConc will never rise above 1667 litres.

This identification of the key factors can be used to decide where the focus of improvements to production can be made. For example, if the quality of the output is not constrained by the quality of a particular component, then there is no benefit in improving the quality of that component.

Linear programming can also be used to carry out sensitivity analysis. Again looking at Figure 4.12, you could calculate how much change in one variable would affect the optimum solution. For example, consider:

◆ Increasing the total output to 5,500 litres. Line (a) would move to the right, so the output of LowConc could be increased by 500 litres, while keeping output of HighConc constant.

◆ Reducing the maximum allowed output of HighConc from 4000 to 3500 litres. This would have no effect on the optimum solution as the output of High Conc is only 3333 litres.

Clearly there are a number of uses for linear programming in production industries. It is also useful in service industries, for example to identify the maximum number of patients that a hospital can treat, based on constraints on the numbers and availabilities of doctors, nurses, porters, beds, and so on.

A major benefit is that creating suitable data for a linear programming exercise makes managers think in detail about the factors that affect performance and quality. However, that also highlights the fact that the early stages of linear programming can be time consuming, since a number of relationships must be identified and expressed mathematically.

Activity 11
Operations research techniques

Objective

This activity will help you to assess the use, benefits and limitations of operations research techniques, including linear programming, queuing theory and simulation.

Task

As manager of a long-stay car park site near an international airport, you cater for large numbers of business and holiday passengers who leave their cars with you and travel to the terminals by shuttle bus. Passengers arrive and park in an arrivals area, register at the office and leave their keys. Your staff then drive the cars to a secure area. Just before passengers return, your staff collect the cars and park them in a departures area.

Your key aims are to maximise profits and maximise the number of repeat bookings by ensuring customer satisfaction.

1. You decide to use a linear programming technique to plan how you can maximise the number of cars. What constraints do you need to consider? What do you expect the outcomes of the linear programming could show?

2. A queuing theory approach seems to be very suitable for the situation in the office. What are the key outcomes you are trying to achieve? What are the variables and what approaches to queuing could you try?

3. As a long-term goal, you consider offering only a service to business passengers who have pre-booked, with frequent minibus transport to terminals, valeting services, discounts for company bookings, and so on. To assess the possible benefits and costs, what factors would you consider in running a simulation of the new business?

Feedback

1. Some of the constraints that you could have identified are:

   ◆ the maximum number of car parking spaces

   ◆ the number of spaces in the arrivals and departures areas

   ◆ the number of staff who can drive the cars

   ◆ the number of staff who work at the office counter.

   Assuming that the areas of the secure, arrivals and departure areas are fixed, any one of them may be the limiting factor. It could be useful to carry out a separate linear programming activity just based on those three factors, to ensure that you are making the best use of the space.

   The number of counter staff could also be critical. Passengers are unlikely to book again if they have to wait a long time to register.

   Thinking about the counter staff point highlights two factors that we have not so far considered. First, could advertising encourage more pre-booking, and so reduce counter time? Second, how effectively do they register customers? Would it help if they had further training in using the computer system?

   As we said above: "A major benefit is that creating suitable data for a linear programming exercise makes managers think in detail about the factors that affect performance and quality."

2. The key outcomes are to process customers quickly and accurately. Some of the factors relating to inputs include:

   ◆ variations in customer numbers throughout the day and at different times of the year

   ◆ peaks in numbers when customers arrive in buses from the terminals

   ◆ differences between business passengers (little luggage, probably pre-booked) and holiday makers.

   Some of the options you have are to:

   ◆ vary the number of counter staff

   ◆ separate arrivals from departures

   ◆ deal with pre-booked passengers separately

   ◆ separate registration from payment

   ◆ vary the size of the buses – using frequent, smaller buses could reduce office congestion.

3. You would certainly want to consider the three factors we outlined: frequent minibus transport to terminals, valeting services, and discounts for company bookings. What would you expect the take-up of each service to be? What are the costs?

You could also consider the possibility of upgrading the premises. What would be the costs? How would the changes be likely to affect customer numbers and satisfaction levels? What level of upgrading would be most effective?

The list of possible factors that you need to consider is long. What about the advertising, using the web, devising a self-registration electronic system using credit cards? What trends can be identified in business travel in general, or at this airport? What if there was a sudden rise in the use of video conferencing?

Note that the simulation exercise will have a number of benefits. The process of identifying the variables makes managers assess and analyse current performance. The outcomes will, as in the two-liquids study, identify some variables can be ignored. And, most important, it will identify a number of factors that appear to have the greatest impact. Using that information, managers can then go on to make their decision.

◆ Recap

Assess the use, benefits and limitations of the statistical techniques of index numbers, time series analysis, and correlation and regression analysis

◆ Index numbers are used to compare changes in different items, provided all the calculations use the same base year. They are particularly useful when assessing the average change for a number of items.

◆ Time series analysis is useful where data demonstrates more than one of the following: a trend, seasonal elements, cyclical elements, and random or residual elements.

◆ Two useful tools are moving averages and trend lines.

◆ Scatter diagrams can identify correlation between two variables. The correlation can be shown as a regression line.

◆ Statistical calculations (e.g. using least squares or Pearson product moment) to assess how closely the results correspond the regression line.

Assess the use, benefits and limitations of techniques linked to probability and sampling, including distribution theory and standard deviation, estimation, significance testing and statistical process control

◆ Decision trees are used to analyse the various outcomes of a number of different actions, based on assessments of the probabilities of each outcome.

◆ Random events follow a normal distribution, represented by the mean and the standard deviation.

◆ Based on the number of events in a sample, statistical tables can give information on the probability that a single event will lie within a stated number of standard deviations of the mean.

◆ The size of a sample has a large impact on how accurately the sample reflects the population. To increase the standard error by a factor of 3 the sample size must be increased by a factor of 3^2, or 9.

◆ Estimation involves the opposite process to sampling. Where sampling finds the properties of a small part of a larger population, estimation starts with a sample and applies the properties of the sample to the larger population.

◆ Statistical process control is used with continuous processes. The aim is to distinguish between chance and assignable variations.

◆ Quality controllers define control limits at each stage of the process, based on the theory of probability distributions.

Assess the use, benefits and limitations of operations research techniques, including linear programming, queuing theory and simulation

◆ Queuing theory looks at the range of variables that can affect a queue, and predicts the likely outcomes.

◆ The key factors to consider in a queuing system are the distribution of arrival times, the distribution of service times, the number of servicing units, and their configuration.

◆ Simulations are used to assess the effects of many variables, where the effects of the variables can only be predicted.

◆ To test the validity of a simulation model, it is usual to run historic data and assess whether the model accurately predicts changes that actually occurred.

◆ Linear programming involves identifying all the factors that act on constraints on an activity and using them to find the optimum outcome (or outcomes).

♦ Linear programming is also used to carry out sensitivity analysis, assessing the affect of making a change to one of the constraints or variables.

▶▶ More @

♦ The range of suitable statistics textbooks is vast. Three useful examples that give detailed descriptions of the techniques in this theme are:

- Owen, F and Jones, R. (1994) *Statistics*, Pitman

- Wisniewski, M. (1997) *Quantitative Methods for Decision Makers*, Pitman

- Buglear, J. (2005) *Quantitative Methods for Business: The A-Z of QM*, Elsevier

Note that, of those three books, only Wisniewski covers Linear Programming, though you can find more on this topic in:

- Swift, L. (2005) *Quantitative Methods for Business, Management and Finance*, Palgrave Macmillan

- Wild, R. (2000) *Production and Operations Management*, Thomson

♦ To review, or upgrade, your understanding of the key mathematics involved in this theme, see Buglear (above):

- Barnett, R.A., Ziegler, M.R. & Byleen, K.E. (2005) *Finite Mathematics for Business, Economics, Life Sciences and Social Sciences*, Prentice Hall.

- Swift, L. (2005) *Quantitative Methods for Business, Management and Finance*, Palgrave Macmillan

♦ Dretke, B.J. (2001) *Statistics with Microsoft® Excel* Prentice Hall
A very useful guide to carrying out the techniques using a commonly available spreadsheet program.

References

Barnett, R.A. Ziegler, M.R. & Byleen, K.E. (2005) *Finite Mathematics for Business, Economics, Life Sciences and Social Sciences*, Prentice Hall.

Bedward, D. and Stredwick, J. (2004) *Managing Information: Core Management*, Elsevier

Buckley, P. and Clark, D. (2004) *A Rough Guide to the Internet*, Rough guides

Buglear, J. (2005) *Quantitative Methods for Business: The A-Z of QM*, Elsevier

Dretke, B.J. (2001) *Statistics with Microsoft® Excel*, Prentice Hall

Ennis, R.H. (1987), 'A taxonomy of critical thinking dispositions and abilities,' in Baron, J.B. and Sternberg, R.J. (Eds), *Teaching Thinking Skills: Theory and Practice*, W. H. Freeman and Co., New York (Quoted in Greenawalt)

Greenawalt, M.B. 'The internal auditor and the critical thinking process,' *Managerial Auditing Journal* 12/2/1997

Guiliani, R. (2003) *Leadership*, Time Warner paperbacks

Informix (1999) 'Executive Summary' Quoted by A.Read 'Managers making dicey decisions' *Internal Auditor*, 12/1/1999

Kerr, M. 'Knowledge Management' *The Occupational Psychologist*, 48, May 2003.

McKenna, E.F. (1996) *Business Psychology and Organisational Behaviour*, Psychology Press

Nickerson, R. C. (2001) 2nd edition, *Business and Information Systems*, Prentice Hall

Nokes, S. (2003) *The Definitive Guide to Project Management: The Fast Track to Getting the Job Done on Time and on Budget*, Prentice Hall

Owen, F and Jones, R. (1994) *Statistics*, Pitman

Robson, W. (1997) *Strategic Management and Information Systems*, Prentice Hall

Swift, L. (2005) *Quantitative Methods for Business, Management and Finance*, Palgrave Macmillan

Wild, R. (2000) *Production and Operations Management*, Thomson.

Wilson, D. A. (2002) *Managing Information: IT for Business Process* **Butterworth-Heinemann**

Wisniewski, M. (1997) Quantitative Methods for Decision Makers Pitman

ENFO, the Irish Department of the Environment and Local Government (www.enfo.ie/leaflets/bs25.htm)

Information Week (www.informationweek.com)

Better Management (www.bettermanagement.com)

Wikepedia (http:en.wikipedia.org)

Skymark (http://www.skymark.com/resources/tools/ pareto_charts.asp)

Top Gear, BBC, September 2006